JENNIFER LAYER

Who the F*ck Am I?

THE PEOPLE PLEASER'S
GUIDE TO SELF-LOVE

KIND OF CATHARTIC PRESS

*Book design by **Jennifer Stimson***

Published by **Kind of Cathartic Press LLC**

www.kindofcathartic.com

Dear 10-year-old Jenny,

You are already everything you will ever need to be.

Yours truly,

26-year-old Jenny

Table of Contents

Introduction

Hi. My name is Jennifer, and I'm an alcoholic.

Just kidding! I'm actually a people pleaser, but I might as well treat this like an AA meeting because people pleasing has sabotaged my life and my relationships nearly as badly as the liquor bottle has for many folks.

I used to think a people pleaser was just someone who couldn't say no to others. While this is a common pattern for us people pleasers, it's not even close to the real definition. The definition I like best is quoted from *Psychology Today* author Dr. Leon F Seltzer who suggests that people pleasers "regard their value in life as based on their value to others."

In other words, a people pleaser understands their self-worth through how well they please other people.

In many cases, society loves people pleasers. I mean, who would argue against a person who lives their life in service to the people around them? In fact, the surface-level characteristics of a people pleaser are often considered ideal and commendable qualities by societal standards.

For example, we tend to give off the impression of being friendly, cooperative, loyal, generous, hardworking, happy, encouraging, and supportive. But underneath this personality display, we are actually severely insecure, desperate, lonely, paranoid, exhausted, self-critical, obsessive, and unsure of who we really are.

Not so appealing anymore, is it?

Recognizing the psychology and reasoning driving these seemingly "good qualities" is where the work for us really begins. At least that's where the work started for me. I always saw my people pleasing as a valuable and positive part of who I was, until one stressful evening when I sat on a little blue cloth couch clutching a decorative pillow to my chest and told the guy sitting across from me that I was spiraling.

Looking at the floor I told him, "I made a mistake at work today. It wasn't even a big deal, but it feels like a big deal. I'm just so mad at myself and upset about this whole stupid day. I cried in the bathroom and yelled at myself in the car. I feel like such a loser. I know I'm being dramatic, but I can't help it."

My therapist responded, "Well that doesn't surprise me. You are an approval seeker. You're addicted to it. So, it makes sense that when that approval is threatened, you respond in anger and fear."

I thought to myself: *That's the dumbest thing I've ever heard. I'm not addicted to anything. I am just emotional. What an idiot.*

I was, of course, in deep denial. But ironically denial is the first step in getting to acceptance, which I eventually reached sitting behind the steering wheel of my little Jeep on the way home from that therapy session. *Dang.* I thought. *He actually might be on to something.*

In putting a label on my overreaction to making a mistake at work, my therapist helped me recognize that for as long as I could remember, my life revolved around getting approval from others by doing whatever it took to please them. Making other people happy is what I lived for. I believed trying hard to please people is what made me a "good" person.

I thought pleasing others was how I made and kept my friends, how I got good grades, how I kept my father around, how I kept my mother from being sad, how I found love, and how I made it through my day undamaged.

However, after doing some research and even more

soul-searching, I found out that my insatiable compulsion to please other people was actually a suffocating and toxic addiction that negatively skewed my sense of self-worth.

Addictions are more than physical dependencies to drugs. The definition of addiction is a biopsychosocial disorder characterized by compulsive engagement in rewarding behaviors despite adverse consequences.

Those rewarding, yet ultimately destructive behaviors can be almost anything: self-harming, gossiping, being sick, watching TV, complaining, overeating, counting calories, sleeping, making money, spending money, instigating drama, having sex with strangers, eating cheese, watching porn, stealing things, adrenaline rushes; the list goes on and on.

But in my case, I became subconsciously addicted to getting other people's approval in order to validate my sense of self-worth. This role often involved me changing who I was, lying to people, doing things I wasn't okay doing, trying to "save" or control people, letting painful actions against me slide, refusing to ask for help, and just about anything I could do to keep other people happy and make them like me.

On that post-therapy car ride home, I had to come to terms with my truth: I was an addict. With this realization came the new goal: I had to reclaim control of my life and figure out how to change these patterns I created that may have felt like safe choices to make but just beneath the surface were silently ruining my life.

But changing life-long established patterns is honestly just as freaking difficult as it sounds.

This addiction to pleasing people was not something I just picked up one day, tried out, and was instantly hooked on.

Despite what Daren the DARE Lion says, keeping yourself addiction free is a lot harder than, "Just saying no." Sometimes you don't even mean to say "yes."

Those of us not actively practicing witchcraft never intentionally mean to invite a demon into our lives. Sometimes it just sneaks up on us in little, tiny bits. The demon shows up as a friend, and we trust it. Being with this friend makes us feel better. It makes us feel safe and protected. So, we allow in or even start to seek bigger bits, until reaching for that demon becomes the only way we know how to survive our lives.

People pleasing was a defense mechanism I built during my childhood in an attempt to gain the acceptance, affection, and presence of the adults in my life. Given that these vital needs were not consistently met in my childhood, I was not able to develop a secure attachment style, nor an accurate image of who I was and how I deserved to be treated by both myself and others.

When the adults in my life were physically absent, emotionally neglectful, unapproachable, inconsistent, or simply unavailable to connect with me, I thought it was my fault. All I saw was that I was not good enough, and thus I developed a habitual pattern of needing to overcompensate for my lack of value by constantly fulfilling the needs and desires of everyone around me.

Further, when my desperate attempts to please people still did not ensure the acceptance, affection, and presence I needed from them, it only further reinforced what I came to see as my own worthlessness. This cause and effect became a tumultuous cycle of putting myself down while trying to lift everyone else up.

In *Psychology Today*, Dr. Seltzer wrote, "People pleasers—so adept at nurturing those around them—literally don't know how to nurture themselves. And because safeguarding relationships is the way they've learned to bolster their fragile egos, they're unable to recognize that the ultimate cost of devoting themselves to the welfare of others is nothing less than sacrificing their own selfhood. Viewing their worth and personal security as totally hinging on pleasing or placating others, they end up forgetting who they are and what they themselves need to feel fulfilled."

It certainly was eye-opening to discover that I did not have the skills to love myself at all. Learning this insight about myself was one thing but figuring out how to step away from these ingrained patterns and instead create new patterns that effectively allowed me to love myself was an entirely different kind of journey.

However, I decided that no matter how painful or terrifying the journey was, it had to be worth it. I knew with some patience and some hard work I could reach outward for knowledge and tools and then look inward to slowly chip away at this chaotic and self-destructive tree that took root in my being.

But as you can imagine, the path of breaking down toxic patterns is not a light switch that is easily flipped. It is a process that is cultivated and a path that is followed while it is being created.

Sure, it's a tough road to go down, but isn't that half the fun of being human? We get to decide who we are. We get to decide how we respond to what we know, especially after having new experiences. How awesome is it that we have the power to change our own lives?

In her book, *You Are a Badass,* Jen Sincero wrote, "It's not your fault that you're fucked up. It's your fault if you stay fucked up."

After admitting to myself that my therapist was right and recognizing that I had some healing to do, I decided to dig deep, face myself, and figure out what my most unhealthy patterns were as a result of this "disease to please" (as coined by Dr. Harriet Braiker).

Over the next three years, I tracked and analyzed the inner workings of my emotional triggers, compulsive thoughts, and unmet needs in order to clearly define what these patterns were, why they existed, how they hurt me, and how to unravel their hold on me.

Each chapter of this book covers a separate pattern and concludes with *Acts of Self-Love* you can practice to aid in your own journey of overcoming similar toxic patterns.

My Top People Pleasing Patterns

1. *I Am Unworthy:* I am self-conscious and self-critical, particularly in social settings. I project these negative self-evaluations onto the people around me, both judging them and feeling judged by them. I subconsciously believe they will deem me unworthy of their time, attention, and love.

2. *I'll Be Whoever You Want Me to Be:* I make my life choices to fit within other people's expectations of who I "should" be.

3. *I Can Save You:* I feel as though I can and must save other people from themselves and their problems. I feel responsible for the feelings and behaviors of others.

4. ***I Need You:*** I am dependent on my relationships with others to validate my sense of self-worth. This causes me to stress over the needs of others while fully neglecting my own, and it keeps me from being able to leave relationships even when they become unhealthy. This pattern is commonly associated as a symptom of an "anxious attachment style."

5. ***I Am Alone:*** I avoid acknowledging and facing negative emotions. I lean on passive aggression and am terrified of direct confrontation. This fear manifests into hiding from people, lying about how I feel, and an overwhelming sense of loneliness.

6. ***I Am Sorry:*** Self-compassion and self-forgiveness do not come easily to me. I am extremely critical of myself and my mistakes. I hold grudges against myself and am my own worst bully.

7. ***I Don't Know Who I Am:*** My authentic self gets lost in the depths of my emotions and the emotions of those around me. I forget who I am and allow myself to fall victim to toxic inner thoughts and toxic communication from others.

If even one of these patterns resonates with you, then dang it, you have some work to do.

Some disclaimers:

1. Throughout this book I will use words like *God, demons, prayer, faith,* etc., because I am a spiritual person, and I made a promise to not change my story to try and be more digestible to the larger public. However, I've also done my very best to not make this a religious book, because again, the intention of the book is not for you to find love outside of yourself, but rather within yourself. So, with that in

mind, I suggest you see words like these as a metaphor for whatever you need them to be. Make this book work for you so you can get something, anything, out of it.

2. Also, I should probably warn you, as often as I drop a "God" bomb, I drop double the F-bombs.

3. While I may not yet be a technically licensed expert in the science of human development, I am an expert of myself and the pursuit of changing my own life. As such, in this book don't expect me to refer to any scientific studies I've conducted, data I've collected, or scriptures I've read. This isn't that kind of book.

This book is me, dissected and displayed on every single page. Just little ol' me sitting in the sharing circle, holding the talking stick, and sharing with you what becoming the person I want to be looks like in my life.

4. There is a key to this whole "becoming someone" journey that I should warn you about. It has no end. "Becoming the person I want to be" is something I can never fully accomplish. As Michelle Obama says, I will always be in the stage and process of "becoming." I will never be anyone's definition of perfect, nor will I ever be exactly everything I dream of. I will always have some growing to do.

Acknowledging the simple fact that perfection is not possible is an important step in being able to take on a journey of "personal development," without getting burnt-out, feeling inadequate, or allowing shame to creep in. To kid yourself into thinking that any future version of yourself could possibly "have it all figured out" is a fool's game in which you always lose.

5. If you're already starting to feel a little overwhelmed by all of this, don't worry, you're not alone. In fact, in the very sense that you may feel lonely in your life, I am right there with you. All alone, together. Just getting through each day, breath by breath.

Some of us are able to reach a place of total and complete serenity with who we are and the life we lead. But as many thought leaders suggest, those people are only monks and sociopaths. As for the rest of us, we all fight constantly to be someone worth being.

6. When you're done reading this book, don't expect to be "fixed" or to never make a self-destructive mistake again. Instead expect to have new insights into how you show up for yourself and new tools to help you do so in a healthier way than you may have in the past. Plan to be guided away from reaching for the wrong solutions, so you can set your sights on values, patterns, and forces that are really worth reaching for.

(Let's pause real quick: after this point, shit gets cringingly personal, so I'm going to take a deep breath. I ask that you take one with me. Breathe in for four seconds, hold it for four seconds, and then let it out. It may seem silly, but do it anyway).

Breathe
All right, let's go.

CHAPTER 1

I Am Unworthy

I am self-conscious and self-critical, particularly in social settings. I project these negative self-evaluations onto the people around me, both judging them and feeling judged by them. I subconsciously believe they will deem me unworthy of their time, attention, and love.

When presented with a significant threat, like a tiger charging at you, the human body will tap into an instinctual fight-or-flight response. During this reaction, a person's heart rate, blood pressure, and breathing increase to prepare them for either fighting off the threat or running away from the threat. Either option will take all the energy a person has.

Anxiety is often described as the fight-or-flight response reacting to an imagined danger. Since you cannot flee from or fight against an imaginary danger, the physical response remains in the body, leaving you with a feeling of low-level panic (aka "anxiety").

(Side note: Exercise is effective at helping calm anxiety because when you move your body, you convince your dumb, instinctual brain that you have successfully deterred or escaped the threat. But unfortunately, we are not always in a situation where we can bust out 50 jumping jacks.)

Anxiety is a feeling that visits me regularly. It gets particularly clingy in social settings. For me, the imagined threat causing this anxiety is that of other people's judgments.

I am, or at least was, acutely obsessed with what other people think about me. If I walked into a room and made eye contact with someone, I immediately assumed that they were judging me. Maybe they thought my hair looked stupid or I did my eye liner wrong. Or maybe they could see into my soul and realized what a loser I really was. I was terrified of being around other people, because when I was, I bullied myself inside my head.

I thought to myself, "No one here likes me. My laugh is stupid. That joke I said was so bad. Everyone can see how much I'm sweating, and they're disgusted. I'm disgusting. I shouldn't be here. I need to leave. I need to disappear."

I wanted to run away from other people's judgments, but since their judgments were just something I imagined in my head and not a real physical danger, I had nowhere to run.

My critical thoughts were not always about me either. Whenever I saw similar "flaws" in other people, I talked mad shit about them in my head. It gave me a false sense of superiority and comfort because their flaw meant I had some sort of power over them.

It's funny how the fear of judgment makes you judgmental. But the deep-rooted insecurity that causes a fear of judgment encourages you to protect yourself by seeking out flaws in others, so you can feel better about yourself and more secure in your being.

I was almost never outwardly judgmental, but internally I was giving nothing by eye rolls and dirty looks. This constant state of negativity going on in my head had a way of harshing my mellow and ruining any good time I was having. This mind set I carried around made any moment involving other people hard for me to enjoy.

Anxiety sculpted me into an introverted person. I preferred solitary activities or being with a few select people rather than seeking out large gatherings or interacting with strangers of any kind. There were just too many opportunities for people to judge me in public.

I hadn't always been this way. Thinking back, my anxiety problems began to flourish in middle school. I think being a middle schooler is hard for everyone. It's just a weird age when you feel emotions you don't understand; you have influences pulling you different ways. And you have to figure out what kind of person you want to be while trying out a bunch of terrible outfits, like my lime green, fishnet, fingerless gloves.

Not to mention, in middle school, my home life was unstable and chaotic, I needed prescription grade deodorant, I had pimples, frizzy hair, and crushes on the worst people. I spent most of my time sitting in class, in the gym, or at lunch, hoping to just disappear. It was more than not wanting to be at school, I didn't want to be at all.

I wasn't suicidal or anything, but I was definitely lost, sad, and filled with relentless anxiety. I just wished I could fade away into the background and did my very best to do just that. I had a constant feeling like no matter where I was, who I was with, or what I was doing, I just didn't belong.

I spent those years living with a sort of constant stage fright. Walking through the hallway, talking to a friend, sitting in class, riding the bus, and just existing outside of my home felt as terrifying as being on a stage in front of people. I often felt very out of place and uncomfortable, like I was one word, one step, one bad move away from being booed out of the building.

However, my true, authentic self or "inner child" is loud, bold, and very high-energy. My authentic self feels no shame for who she is and really just wants to explore and connect with people. But when I was with other people and this authentic part of me came out, it brought up a sense of shame and fear within me.

I wanted to be loud, funny, and obnoxious, but hated myself any time I acted that way because I was terrified that people were judging me. My authentic self and my approval-seeking self were at war with each other constantly. Over time, the approval-seeking-self won, and my authentic self was stuffed into a mental closet and only allowed out at certain times of the day.

My toxic inner dialogue taunted me constantly. "I'm so ugly, no wonder boys never talk to me. Just stop talking already; people hate the sound of my voice. My artwork sucks, people will laugh at me for making it."

This inner dialogue followed me into high school, college, and my working life as an adult. It followed me into every club I joined, every sport I played, every piece of art I created, every relationship I entered, the projects I completed, and every single job I have ever had. The anxiety found its way into even the smallest actions, like controlling the aux cord with friends because I was terrified that they'd judge and dislike my musical taste.

There are a lot of different ways you could define this feeling. You could call it social anxiety disorder, imposter syndrome, or low self-esteem. It doesn't matter what you call it. What matters is how I undo the damage these patterns and feelings did to my sense of self-worth.

The constant feeling of being negatively judged is not only exhausting but also toxic. It changes the way you see yourself and the way you see and connect with others. This perspective can make you hate everyone around you and can make you hate yourself as well. You hate everyone for making you feel like you are not good enough and you hate yourself because a part of you believes they are right. This perspective will encourage you to want to change, hide, and break yourself down to be reshaped into someone who *is* good enough.

And so, for me, the self-hate accumulated. I hated my nose, my stomach, my laugh, my voice, my brain, my clothes, my dance moves, my face, my body, my personality, and myself.

It was nearly impossible for me to feel loved by other people because I didn't think I deserved their love in the first place. I was all together just not good enough.

Deep down, this belief was a defense mechanism I created to protect myself from the heartbreak of being neglected and abandoned. If you never allow yourself the chance to feel loved by others, then it hurts less when they take that love away. (Talk about Daddy issues, am I right? But we'll get to that later.)

My subconscious-self believed that as long as I continued to accept that I wasn't worthy of love, I would be safe from other people hurting me. If I hurt myself first, they would never even get the chance to. This way of thinking somehow gave me a sense of control over my life and my emotions.

Not all people respond to self-judgment the same way that I did. Many respond with extreme over-confidence and anger/belittlement towards everyone around them. However, these reactions fight the same underlying battle.

When I was emotionally and physically neglected as a child, I began to associate the pain I felt with my own lack of worth. I believed my needs were not met because I wasn't worthy of other people's love. There was just something inherently wrong with me. This feeling of shame telling me that there was something deeply wrong with me, crept up in all areas of my being. Nothing I did, said, wore, created, or felt was ever good enough.

I was not good enough.

I was simply unworthy.

So, I started serving other people to feel worthy of their love. I was not worthy on my own and had to become someone else for them. Other people's love was conditional. My worth was conditional. My worth had to be earned, proven, and validated through pleasing other people, even if I was secretly judging them.

That is, until one day on the therapy couch, I learned an earth-shattering truth: *my worth is unconditional.*

You may think this message is some regurgitated, hippie nonsense I read off a cat poster on some little girl's wall. But stick with me.

First off, the idea of unconditional worth is not acceptable in today's society. The reality is, most of society will die behind the idea that our worth is 100% conditional.

Society will say a person's worth is conditional on how happy they are, their actions, kindness, work ethic, wealth, health, height, education, mindfulness, character, how many push-ups they can do, how many friends they have, how often they volunteer, what politician they voted for, how many good deeds they do a day, how well-behaved their kids are, how clean their house is, how many hours of sleep they get a night, how satisfying their job is, their follower count, eating habits, and just about anything a company can put a dollar sign behind and convince them will increase their worth as a human being.

Modern life will convince you, as it did me, that you are broken, ugly, and too fucked up to be worth anything. Then society will step in and convince you that it's okay, because you can become someone who does have worth if you simply change everything about yourself. Society will convince you that you need to increase your value as a human being to thus increase your chances of being loved. But this book is not about changing society; it's about changing you. You are the only one who has to believe in your worth for it to become a guiding reality in your life.

Personally, this whole idea of unconditionality was extremely difficult for me to wrap my head around. I just didn't understand a world in which my worth was not the direct result of power, money, beauty, good behavior, or how well I pleased and impressed the people around me. I thought my worth was completely conditional on doing "good girl things" and becoming the kind of person that people loved.

While the concept took me some time to accept, I've come to learn that my worth is not dependent on *any*thing. I can hate myself all I want to. Other people can hate me too. I can mess up, let people down, embarrass myself, fall on my face, be dumb, ugly, sad, mean, lonely, and lazy.

While we're at it, let's cross the line and go way overboard with it. I can be a sadistic, abusive, racist, homophobic, serial killer, with a bad attitude, funky armpit B.O., middle fingers tattooed on my eyelids, and any other immoral, deplorable, nauseating, or villainous description you can think of. And even still… I will have worth and will be worthy of love. When I say unconditional, I mean it. No exceptions.

Whoa, whoa, whoa. You may be thinking, *hey now, that's drifting into evil people territory, and I refuse to vibe with that.* And that's okay. Keep reading anyways.

There is a discrepancy of word choice I need to clarify. <u>Love</u>, and the ability to healthily give and receive it within yourself and with others, <u>is absolutely conditional</u>. Love is such a complex concept, of which I cannot claim any real answers to. Love is difficult. It fluctuates, takes extreme effort to grow and maintain, varies in its degrees, and is ten thousand percent conditional on how you think, feel, and treat people.

On the other hand, while love itself is extremely conditional, your worth is not. <u>Your worth</u>, or the "light" that exits within you exists unconditionally. The degree to which you deserve to receive, feel, and give love, whether or not you are currently doing so or even able to, <u>is unconditional</u>.

Every single last human being on this planet, no matter how fucked-up you may think they are, or how fucked-up they actually are, has unconditional worth and value, including you.

You are a light, whether you are living into and spreading that light or not. You have worth whether you believe it or not.

Now I'm absolutely **not** condoning bad behavior out here. I'm not saying it's okay to be any of the awful things I listed on the previous page. I'm not saying you should settle for being a terrible person because in the end you're still "a light" and you'll still "be worthy of love."

No. Actually, the exact opposite. If you decide to live a pathetic and twisted life, absent of love, filled with hurtful judgements of yourself and others, shitty behavior, truly selfish choices, and an inability to let yourself be happy or be who you really are, you will have completely wasted your gift of unconditional worth.

You will die having rejected the most awesome part of being human, which is that at any stage of your life, you get to decide who you are and how you show up in this world. You have value and worth no matter what, so therefore you should not waste that gift of grace.

It is because of the absolute unconditionality of your worth that you should do everything in your power to see and embrace the light that is you. You should, and perhaps desperately need to, start taking ownership of your life. You must take responsibility for your choices, how you treat yourself, and how you treat others, so you can create a life for yourself, filled with the love of which you <u>have always</u> and <u>will always</u> be worthy of holding.

For me, taking ownership of my life meant revising my victim mentality to one of gratitude and self-compassion. This change required reevaluating my judgmental attitude and working to end the war going on inside of my head. It meant accepting myself for exactly who I am. It meant getting dressed in the mirror and falling deeply in love with the girl looking back at me.

Revising my perspective meant going to a party and choosing to believe that not only were people enjoying my presence, but also believing that even if they weren't, it didn't matter. It meant reprogramming my brain to learn how to love myself.

Recognizing the unconditionality of your worth also requires you to realize the power you have over your own life. This journey of growth will look different for each person. For some, growth may mean going to a therapist, or dare I say it, even a psychiatrist.

For others, the journey could mean going into the woods for a year to do nothing but self-reflection (a drastic reaction, but possibly effective). The point is everyone's journey is different. But the one thing we all have in common is that we are in charge of our own journeys. No one else can make you see your worth. That value is a gift only you can give yourself.

This book will not make you love yourself. I will not make you love yourself. Your mom, your spouse, nor your dog can make you love yourself. Only you can give yourself the gift of self-love.

I spent so many years of my life surrounded by love from others, but I never felt it because I was not convinced of my worth. I didn't even want to be around people at all because I was so convinced that I wasn't worthy of their time, attention, or affection. I was unable to feel love from other people because I needed a foundation of self-love to make that possible.

Nothing on Earth can fill the space in your soul that is reserved for self-love. It is necessary for internal and external growth. It is vital to the quality of your external relationships and ultimately, your contentment in this life.

Realizing and actualizing your self-worth through self-love is the soil from which all your other relationships will grow. If you don't have the soil, the foundation, the place to start from, nothing will grow for very long. You can be so deeply in love with someone, but if you don't have a sturdy foundation of self-love and an understanding of your value, the love they give you will not be enough.

Sometimes, I think back on what I used to say to myself in the mirror, how I used to treat my body, and how I caved into giving people anything they asked for, even if it was my body. It was through those actions that I created this pit of seeming emptiness and constant anxiety.

Instead of building a sturdy foundation of self-love, I dug a deep hole of shame, self-pity, and desperation. Anytime someone even stuck a toe into my pit, I grabbed them and threw them in. I needed them to fill the void I created. I clung so hard to people, gave them anything they wanted, and didn't care how they treated me. I may have not even liked them, but I still needed them to like me. And I hated myself for feeling so desperate.

I spent a lifetime reaching for the wrong things. I thought forces outside of myself, like love and approval from others was the goal, the answer that would fill this void inside of me. But those never worked. The void was never truly filled by how much attention or praise I was given, how many hours I volunteered, how much I prayed, the money I made, trips I took, emotions I bottled up, miles I ran, relationships I cultivated, or friendships I had. It took me a long, long time to realize, but the void had to be filled in by me, loving me, unconditionally.

Learning how to love myself was (and is) not an easy process. I had no idea that I could fill the void myself. I didn't know I could even create love for myself.

Once I learned how to embrace the unconditionality of my worth, little by little, I was able to recognize my negative self-talk for what it was: a defense. And a really piss-poor one at that. I began to feel okay being around other people, specifically strangers. I was able to have fun at a party, instead of feeling overwhelmed by made-up thoughts in my head of what other people thought of me. I was able to connect with others, without feeling the insatiable urge to make them laugh, service a need, fuel their ego, or in any way make them feel good. Connecting with others was no longer about making them happy so they could validate me but was more about just wanting to connect. It was about allowing our lights to be seen by each other. It was simple.

Choosing to believe that my worth is unconditional has transformed the way my brain functions. This decision has fully changed the way I connect with others and what I even believe "love" to be. The belief has allowed me to write this book without drowning in the overwhelm of people potentially hating it or just the idea of people knowing so much about my personal life.

In choosing to believe in the unconditionality of your worth, you will slowly learn to stop caring about what other people might think about you because you'll know your worth is not dependent on what they think. Your worth is not even dependent on what *you* think. Your worth will exist whether you or anyone else believes in it or not. And so, as cliché and obnoxious as this truth sounds, the very first step in figuring out self-love is recognizing that you're worthy of love in the first place.

Acts of Self-Love to Practice

1. Get Out of Your Dang Head

The best advice my mom ever gave me was to stop believing the stories I made up in my head. To be sane, and especially to be self-loving, you have to know the difference between what's real and what's not.

One of the ways I worked on recognizing what was true was to write down my thoughts, also called journaling.

When I was convinced that my boyfriend didn't really love me, or that my boss was going to fire me, or that I was going to fail a test, or that my friends were talking about me behind my back, I took out my notebook and wrote out all the stories in my head that led me to these hurtful conclusions.

Once I got it all out on paper, I read it back to myself. Then, sentence by sentence I determined whether or not that sentence was a fact of truth or a story I made up. Doing this exercise helped me realize what gigantic leaps I made from a minor truth to an ultimately self-destructive, made-up conclusion.

For example:

Sentence 1: My partner told me the house is a mess.

Sentence 2: They don't appreciate me and think I'm a bad partner.

Sentence 3: I am a bad partner.

Sentence 4: They are a bad partner.

Sentence 5: Our relationship is doomed.

When these thoughts are in my head, they all seem like they are valid. But once I write them down, I very quickly see the leaps I made and the lies I told myself. I realize how I project my own fears and insecurities onto other people. I assume other people believe these ideas about me, when in reality, they are all in my head.

However, if you keep these thoughts in your head and don't label them as the lies they are, your subconscious mind will absorb them and internalize them. You will continue with your life, actually believing these absurd thoughts, and you will create a self-fulfilling prophecy of failure, judgment, and bitterness.

So, go grab a journal, open up a Word doc on your computer, or the notes app in your phone and get to writing. Do it once a day, especially when you're feeling stressed, overwhelmed, or any sort of strong, negative, or positive emotion.

2. Change How You Speak to and About Yourself

Your words, whether spoken, silent, or even subconscious have power over you. If you scoff and stick up your nose at the idea of self-affirmations, then I implore you to reconsider.

In his book, *Unfu*k Yourself,* Gary John Bishop explains that while positive self-talk can drastically improve your life, "...the reverse is also true: Negative self-talk can not only put us in a bad mood, but it can also leave us feeling helpless. It can make small problems seem bigger – and even create problems where none existed before. Here's the breaking news, your self-talk is fucking you over and in ways you can't even begin to imagine."

First off, go get Gary's book. It's super short and super helpful.

Second off, stop letting yourself talk down to you. I can't count the number of times I've called myself stupid. Being thought of as stupid is probably my deepest insecurity, to the point that I have nightmares about it. So then, why do I constantly berate myself with such a mean word? All it does is make me feel like shit. It doesn't make me any smarter. Nor does it fix whatever mistake I made that urged me to call myself stupid.

I am not stupid. I am extremely intelligent. But this truth is something I have to verbally remind myself of. I have to catch myself in the slip of saying, "I'm stupid." I have to cut myself off mid-sentence because I am not allowed to talk to myself that way anymore.

There is an app I have downloaded on my smart phone called I Am. I have set it up to give me six affirmational notifications a day. The one that is currently on my screen as I write this says, "I deserve love."

Every time an I Am notification pops up, I repeat it to myself three times. I speak into my consciousness positivity. I affirm myself. I speak good energy into my life.

You don't need an app or a book to do this. This exercise is something you can do all on your own with a little bit of practice. But if you need extra help, please realize how many hundreds of resources there are at your fingertips.

Consistently affirming yourself is a simple act of self-love that will very slowly, over time, change how you see yourself.

Trust me, I know how hard it can be to fight off negative self-talk. Most of the time, those criticisms just slip out unintentionally. But you have to make a conscious effort to control your words.

As long as you begin to make a habit of telling any negativity towards yourself to just fuck off, because actually you're awesome, then you'll be that much closer to creating positive, self-affirming, loving thoughts on a regular basis.

3. Pay Attention to Your Judgments

Most of the time, when you harshly judge other people, that response is stemming from a place of insecurity, not superiority. Recognizing these insecurities can be extremely difficult, but the best way to do so is to just pay attention to the next time you judge someone. Ask yourself, "Is there a quality in them that I see in myself? Do I worry that other people judge me about this same matter?" If the answer is yes, which it most likely is, then try to recognize and face that insecurity.

You'll be surprised how much you can learn about yourself by paying attention to the qualities that bother you in other people.

4. Take Ownership of Your Life

While your worth is unconditional, the benefits reaped through that worthiness are not given, they are earned. Love is worked for, both from others and from yourself. Power, success, contentment, inner peace, mental stability, and joy are all worked for.

But once you realize that you are worthy of all these things, that truth breaks down all the walls.

You and I, although we may survive in dramatically different bodies, cultures, and circumstances, are worth the same. You have just as much claim to your dreams as I do. You are worth just as much as I am. So, claim that worth.

To believe that your worth is truly unconditional, you have to prove it to yourself. Your worth will exist whether you get the life you want or not. So, take ownership of that worth. Take ownership of your life and put in the work.

CHAPTER 2

I'll Be Whoever You Want Me to Be

I make my life choices to fit within other people's expectations of who I "should" be.

Growing up, I was what some might call an eccentric child. When it came to living, I leaned all the way in, stretching my hands out as far as they could reach, and grabbed anything that brushed against my fingertips. No tree went unclimbed. No invasive or impulsive question went unasked. No curious thought went unexplored.

My mindset was to go all-in on every thought and impulse, taking advantage of every moment. For me, this mentality was the only way of living that made any sense. To everyone else, this was totally, fucking exhausting.

During my single-digit years, nearly every time my mom came home from a long day of work, there would be an amazing surprise waiting for her. Either I moved all the furniture in the house to adjust our feng shui, nailed decorations to our walls, carved drawings into our furniture with knives, or cut holes into her favorite pair of shoes because I thought it made them look more stylish. Already exhausted from a long day, these surprises were never cute changes for my mom to come home to.

Anytime we left the house, I ran away from whomever my adult was, mom, grandma, and babysitter alike, seeking out the darkest hallways, shiniest objects, and most climbable furniture. To top it off, I was a fast runner. My caretakers angrily chased after me while I zig-zagged past their attempts to grab me.

As I skated just out of their reach, through big rooms with crowds of people, I screamed out all the funny things I heard that day. For example, in the '90s there was a band called Barenaked Ladies. When little Jennifer found this out, she went screaming, "Barenaked Ladies!" repeatedly as she ran away from her family in the mall. Once they got a hold of me, I fought back. Like actually fought them. With the punching and the kicking and the screaming.

Being contained in any way was my biggest grievance. My covers couldn't be too tight during bedtime, the car seat felt like torture not protection, and don't even think about hugging me. Being restrained meant I couldn't move. And I had to move. All the time. I had so much energy inside me that holding it in and sitting still was simply not an option. Ever.

Sometimes, when I was in bed attempting to sleep, I had a sudden urge to move. So, I quietly got out of bed, made my way to the living room, climbed up the couch to unlock the front-door deadbolt, and ran down the street in my bare feet and Winnie the Pooh PJs.

Sometimes, my hyperactivity got so intense that it evolved into a manic energy episode, much like an engine with all gas pedal and no brake. During these episodes I felt I had to do something huge, audacious, and loud, or I would simply die. These episodes usually looked like me parkouring around the room, bouncing off all surfaces until eventually I hurt myself or broke something.

When such an episode occurred, my mom and brother, after eventually grabbing hold of me, took me by the arms and got me to the couch. I violently swung my fists at them, trying to prevent the containment I knew was coming. They managed to sit down with me on their lap and grabbed my forearms to fold them against my chest. Their legs twisted around my shins to keep me from kicking. And they just held me there for what felt like an eternity in this unshakable, human straight jacket.

Even though this strategy stunted my range of motion, it did not stunt my urge to move. In fact, the opposite. The confinement only exacerbated my urge to move and threw me into panic mode, like a claustrophobic person locked in the trunk of a car. My energy flooded out of me, and I squirmed and screamed for as long as it took me to calm down. Which I always did, eventually.

As exhausting as this battle was for me, I can't imagine how exhausting it was for my mom, who after working a long, hard day at a demanding job just wanted to relax at home and have some quality time with her kids. Only to find me rampaging through the house like a rabid raccoon, frothing at the mouth, ready to bite.

I was not any better behaved at school. Nap time was the biggest joke on the planet. My preschool called my mom so many times to complain about my inability to take a nap that a group of moms got together and went to the school to protest in my defense. "Jennifer doesn't need to sleep. Let her do something else while the others sleep!" The people in my community, especially my grandmother and my mom, gave all they had to give to help me with my energy issues.

I was put into all the extracurricular activities that our neighborhood had to offer. I did gymnastics, horse-back riding, karate, Girl Scouts, cheerleading, theater, soccer, tee-ball, swimming, art club, and just about everything else that was available. They tried different methods of discipline to tame my spirit. They tried all the negative and positive reinforcement techniques that books could provide, all short of physical violence. While some methods helped, none served as a be-all, end-all solution.

As the years went on, my class sizes grew, the assignments got heavier, and recess was no longer half the day. My teachers' tempers grew too short for any group of protective moms to sway.

It was time to start looking for alternatives, because that single mother of two, those worn-out teachers, and that reckless, uncontrollable child needed a solution. And the world presented one. The schools, the doctors, the science, and yes, even child-protective services all reached out their latex-gloved hands, offering a little orange bottle filled with little white pills. I was officially labeled ADHD.

What is ADHD you ask? According to Dale Archer in his book, The ADHD Advantage, "The trait is a combination of brain chemistry and genetics that affect the dopamine transporter gene and its receptors. Simply put... ADHD can be understood as a brain with a very low boredom threshold... The brain reacts differently to stimulation [depending on where you fall on the ADHD spectrum]. People who have it chafe against the mundane and routine. And yet they excel in chaotic situations. Centuries ago, they would have been the restless ones in the village during times of plenty, but when famine or catastrophe struck, they were the fearless leaders who found new lands or new ways of surviving."

But I wasn't facing famine, war, or catastrophe. No, my life was a very blessed and privileged one. I faced something I considered much worse: boredom. I was confronted with classrooms, quiet hours, bedtimes, seat belts, and oh so many fucking rules.

When the medicine was first introduced to my life, I hated it and often refused to take it. My mom had experience with this sort of attitude though, as I also regularly refused to brush my teeth, take baths brush my hair, eat my dinner, or go to sleep. No matter how hard I argued or how profusely I refused, she had her ways of getting me to make the healthy choice.

Still, I had my own ways of rebelling. Each morning, I dejectedly took the pill and pretended to swallow it. I managed to cheek the pills most days. My mom would even make me open my mouth to check that I really swallowed it. But I was pretty good at it. I waited until she left the room, then I spit the pill out and hid it around the house in all the places I thought she would never look.

However, everyone always seemed to know when the pill hadn't been swallowed. Maybe because I was spinning in circles or asking too many irrelevant questions. The adults in my life looked at me exasperatedly and asked, "You didn't take your medicine today, did you?"

This question irked me. The fact that people could always tell the difference and made it so very clear which version of me they liked better In my little undeveloped mind, I never heard a caring question about the status of my dopamine levels; instead I heard, "You are bothering me. Go fix yourself so you are easier to be around."

This constant annoyance people seemed to have with me was irritating and a little hurtful. Like someone poking me in the ribs with a long stick over and over again. But I thought, no matter how bothersome the poking was, it still beat taking those stupid pills. They fucked with my head. They made my insides feel weird. They depressed me. My mind was filled with a flourish of energy, inspiration, emotion, and opportunity. But once I popped that pill in, the world went quiet, and my thoughts stopped moving. It was like someone turned down the dial on my mind. Not to say that my mind was off. It wasn't. But it was slower, quieter, less exciting, and my greatest grievance, restrained.

The pills made it hard for me to feel my emotions. Not like some doped-up robot, but more like a confused little kid fighting against a parasite that was trying to control my mind. Some doctors might say the quieting of emotions is a benefit of ADHD medication. But each body and mind are different, and I'm not convinced that it was a benefit for me.

It was as though all of my emotions were paralyzed, scrunched up, and stuffed deep down into a tiny little box in the back of my mind. I didn't know how to feel anymore, because all my emotions were just one big smushed-up jumble of confusion, which only seemed to manifest into increasing anxiety and a constant miscommunication of how I felt.

Dale Archer claims, "These meds do work, up to a point. They help the executive functions of the brain, such as the ability to anticipate outcomes, make good decisions, suppress emotions, filter impulsive words and gestures, and generally control urges ... [However] It seems we are only just beginning to understand the toll these meds are taking. Animal studies suggest these meds could alter the whole structure and function of the brain increasing anxiety, causing depression, and despite the short-term gains of better focus, ultimately eroding cognitive powers."

After trying the medication the first few times, I quickly decided nope, that's not for me. I don't like it, I don't want it, and I don't need it! My mom tried her best to explain to me why I had been prescribed the medication and how I could personally benefit from taking it, but I didn't care.

I was completely fine with my overactive self. I liked being exactly who I was. I was an adventurer. I was an explorer. I was a creator of art, stories, and imaginary worlds. I was kind (most of the time). I was smart. I was having fun. In short, I liked myself. Why the hell should I take behavioral medication? From my perspective nothing about me needed changing. So, I decided I would just keep on rocking my life without the meds.

Then one day in the fifth grade, after a morning of defiant pill sneaking, I was at my school desk with four desk buddies. One girl - let's call her Sarah - was someone I considered a relatively good friend. As we all worked on some sort of group assignment, we were allowed to get up and move around the desk huddle. The commotion and movement of group work in the room sparked my energy levels.

Recess was coming up soon, so I was mentally geared up for some energy-filled shenanigans. Overwhelmed by all the excitement in the room, I decided recess couldn't wait. So, when Sarah turned her back to me, I grabbed her shoulders and leaped onto her back. She yelled, "Oh my gosh!" and shook me off her body. She turned to face me with furrowed eyebrows and serious anger in her eyes. She shook her head and yelled, "What is wrong with you today? You are *so* annoying. If we are going to sit together, you need to take your medicine!"

I didn't say anything back. I stared at her and in my peripherals could see everyone around us turn to look at me. No one said anything. She turned away with a *humph* and continued with whatever work we were supposed to be doing. I continued standing there, staring now at the wall, too embarrassed to move. My cheeks began to get red hot and I filled to the brim with anger. Eventually I turned away, walked back to my seat, and plopped down in my chair. The assignment was the farthest thing from my mind. I sat there staring into nothing with the occasional angry glare in Sarah's direction. But she purposefully did not look at me.

Anger pumped through my veins and seemed to gather in a massive clump in my chest. I could feel it burning. Then quite suddenly, the burning sensation was replaced with an acute stabbing pain.

That stick everyone kept poking me with seemed to have finally broken through my thick skin. I felt a hole in my chest.

A little melodramatic, you say? You're right, I was. But again, I had a pretty dramatic personality altogether. I was a person who felt every emotion to its extreme. And on that particular day, shame breathed itself into me and flooded my entire body, mind, and spirit.

I don't know what it was about those words, about that moment, or about that friend, but something in my mind officially fell off the ledge I was balancing on. During recess, almost as though I put myself in time-out, I walked to the farthest corner of our acre-sized, fenced-in play area and stared out the black crosswire gate at passing cars. Alone, I sat down in my corner, looking at the rejected bits of myself bleeding out onto the grass and the tears began to trickle down my still-red cheeks.

As I sat crying in my corner, the negative self-talk spilled out like vomit. My friends don't even like me. I just bother people all day long. I am selfish. I am annoying. I hate myself.

When I got home that night, I didn't really talk to anyone. I just kept to myself and went to bed. The next morning as I looked at myself in the mirror, I thought to myself, "Everyone is right. They tried to tell me. But I'm too stupid to listen and too selfish to care. I'm a problem that needs to be fixed."

That same morning, when my mom handed me my pill, I swallowed it. No games, no faking, no lies. And I took that pill every single day for the next 14 years.

Once I got used to the side effects, the pills weren't so bad, actually. I quickly noticed how the adults around me were not as frustrated with me. I noticed that my outbursts and manic episodes were more controllable. I didn't have to fight against my seat in class. I could raise my hand to answer a question and be okay if I wasn't called on. I could watch an entire movie without getting up to do something else. I could go out on the town with my family without them worrying about impending chaos. I could pay attention in a conversation without obsessively thinking about something more interesting. I was finally rid of that insatiable urge to physically move or interrupt people. In short, I had self-control.

The medicine worked. Little crazy Jennifer was cured.

The medicine seemed to improve me. It changed the way I handled myself, controlled my energy and emotions. The people around me began to allow or even welcome my presence. I became a better student, a better daughter, a better friend, and a much better kid to have sitting next to you on a crowded, four-hour, cross-country flight.

I did everything right. I was finally the good girl everyone wanted me to be. Yet somehow, during this time of exponential outward healing and growth in my life, my insides still hurt. The negative self-talk that I first barfed up on the playground that fateful fifth-grade day, still sat like a rock in the pit of my stomach.

Every morning as I got ready for school, I looked at myself in the mirror, stared into my own eyes and thought, I'm pathetic. I'm an embarrassment to myself and to my family. Not good enough. Not good enough. I am not good enough.

Every morning as I swallowed the pill and all my pride along with it, I internalized and spoke into my daily consciousness these thoughts. And thus began a decade-and-a-half battle between my authentic self and my people-pleasing self. Thus began my incessant anxiety of being around other people. Thus began the decline of my self-esteem and sense of self-worth.

I believed that the version of myself that I once loved so much was not only no good, but she was unworthy of love. To be worthy and good, I had to become something and some-one that I wasn't. I had to be quiet. I had to be still. I had to be small. And more important than anything else, I had to be liked. As though other people's approval was the very air I breathed.

I was the same person, just much smaller. Broken down. Smashed up into little pieces so I could fit inside of the pock-ets of the people around me. I lost myself. The me I once was would never have abandoned love for herself in return for love from others. But this new me hated herself in return for love from others.

While taking my medication certainly helped me function at higher levels and allowed me to survive in such a demanding world, it also served as one of the first big steps in relinquishing who I was to please other people. Actually, it was not even a step; it was more like a leap. My first giant leap into creating a lifelong pattern of sacrificing my real needs and true desires to feed my desperate craving for worth, approval, and social acceptance.

Now, to be clear, the physical medication was not the root cause of this tumult within me. After all, the medicine did exactly what it was intended to do: it got me through school. While I also believe the medication did increase my anxiety and depression, this chapter is not about the meds. It's about what the meds represented.

At the core, those pills were a daily physical reminder to myself that the comfort of others mattered more than my own. They reminded me that I was "supposed to" fill everyone else's cup while completely neglecting my own.

Let's not misinterpret this to say that taking medication on the advice of our loved ones and medical care professionals is "neglecting our needs for the sake of others." For many people living their best life often requires them to take medication that they don't think they need and that they don't want to take.

But it is also critical to remember that we are individuals and not a communal "diagnosis." All of our needs are different and when I took my medication, it didn't make me feel better. It calmed me down, sure. But calmness wasn't necessarily what I needed, it was simply what was demanded of me from an overcrowded and underfunded educational system, and over-worked, frustrated, and mentally exhausted caretakers. I didn't take the medication for myself; I took it for everyone else.

I eventually grew to believe that my value in this world was completely dependent on how well I pleased the people around me. And since I couldn't please the people around me without my medication, I felt as though I had no value without it. Which, you have to admit, is a pretty miserable and unsettling way to see yourself at nine years old.

I didn't verbally tell myself that I was worthless, but I only took the medication because I believed I was. Eventually, taking the medication became a ritual behavior that I didn't even question or think twice about. It was no different than brushing my teeth every morning. Yet, the feeling of not being good enough also became a ritual feeling. A thought that I was able to stuff down deep inside and pretend wasn't a problem. A feeling I didn't talk about or even acknowledge. It was just always there, deep in the back of my mind. Lurking.

Every now and then, I tried telling people about the thoughts in my head and the negative emotions I seemed to constantly have. But I was confused and never able to communicate about my feelings accurately. It was extremely difficult for me to shine a light on my problems because I wanted people to think I was perfect. I wanted people to be proud of me, not worried about me. So, I didn't put that much effort into reaching out.

There were many times growing up that I considered throwing the medicine away. But that voice in the back of my head wouldn't let me. She said, "No, the real me is an annoying, rejected, failure of a person. The real me makes people angry. The real me will not find love. I am not a safe person to be."

No amount of conscious belief within myself could quiet this voice. The voice, that no matter how well I did in life, kept reminding me that I still wasn't good enough. The voice that told me my purpose was not to find love within myself but to gain value only through how much other people loved me.

In college, my daily anxiety got so severe that I ended up struggling with chronic insomnia. I googled what to do about my lack of sleep and saw a website that suggested therapy. I had free counseling available through my university, so I decided to give it a shot. This is the point where everything changed. Not to be overly dramatic here, but therapy saved me.

It took many years of hard work, patience, research, and divine intervention to get to a point where I could function off my medication. And I don't mean function in just the technical sense, but more importantly function in the sense that I didn't loathe who I was unmedicated.

This journey of self-actualization was much less about the physical act of taking medication and much more about dropping the desire to fit into a life that had been prescribed for me. A life in which I hid myself to become the person I was "supposed" to be.

I had to recognize and disconnect from my original life's goal: to please everyone else. I had to recognize that the person I was at my core, the loud, obnoxious, thrill-seeker who can't sit still in her seat, was good enough for me. That little girl I used to love so much was good enough for me. I didn't need to change for anyone. If there were people in my life who couldn't handle me in my truest form, then that was their problem and their loss, not mine.

Jen Sincero said, "You are perfect. To think anything less is as pointless as a river thinking that it's got too many curves or that it moves too slowly or that its rapids are too rapid. Says who? You're on a journey with no defined beginning, middle, or end. There are no wrong twists and turns. There is just being. And your job is to be as you as you can be. This is why you're here. To shy away from who you truly are would leave the world you-less. You are the only you there is and ever will be. I repeat, you are the only you there is and ever will be. Do not deny the world its one and only chance to bask in your brilliance."

A long time ago, I talked with my brother about how I wanted to lower my medication dosage, but I wasn't getting the appropriate advice I needed from my psychiatrist. In that moment, he said something so powerful and incredibly eye-opening to high-school Jennifer, "Then decide for yourself. No one can tell you what's right for you. Not mom, not me, not even a doctor, because no one can be in your body and in your mind and know how you feel. You have to decide what's right for you. It's your body and your life."

It only took six more years for his advice to sink in.

Please don't misunderstand me. I am not poo-pooing on listening to our doctors, accepting advice, or taking medication of any kind. My point is that as an adult, your decisions are your own. As a child, I didn't really have a choice as to how I was cared for. After all, I was not my own responsibility; I was the responsibility of others, so they had to make decisions for me to care for me the best way they could. As I got older, the responsibility shifted to me, yet I still based my decisions and actions on what other people thought I should do.

When I first decided to try and get off my medication, I had many different people tell me that it was a bad idea and would potentially ruin the life that I had worked so hard to create for myself. I had to take in this feedback and still make the choice that I felt was right for me.

Now I live into who I am instead of who other people want me to be. Sure, I embarrass myself from time to time. I'm a little more impulsive, chatty, and bold. Sure, I have a constant stream of energy and have to carry a fidget cube with me at all times. I am a lot more honest and open than I have ever been and maybe say more than I should to the wrong people. But that is who I am. And who I am is pretty freaking awesome if you ask me.

In her book, Girl, Wash Your Face, Rachel Hollis wrote, "I cannot continue to live as half of myself simply because it's hard for others to handle all of me." In reading this quote, I realized what real dangers lurked in my "disease to please." The danger was that pleasing others forced me to only live half a life. By constantly holding myself back and breaking myself down to be better for everyone else, I could lose the person I authentically am in the process. And that is not the life I want to live. I want to be all of me.

I choose to be all of me.

Acts of Self-Love to Practice

1. Embrace Vulnerability

In her book, *The Gifts of Imperfection,* Brené Brown wrote, "We cultivate love when we allow our most vulnerable and powerful selves to be deeply seen and known, and when we honor the spiritual connection that grows from that offering with trust, respect, kindness and affection… Embracing our vulnerabilities is risky but not nearly as dangerous as giving up on love and belonging and joy—the experiences that make us the most vulnerable. Only when we are brave enough to explore the darkness will we discover the infinite power of our light."

I think the concept of vulnerability is different to different folk. To some it may mean crying actual tears for the first time in your adult life. It could mean looking at yourself naked in the mirror or washing off your makeup in front of someone you like. To some, vulnerability looks like admitting you need help and reaching out to a doctor, therapist, spiritual leader, or loved one. To some, vulnerability means telling someone that deep, dark, shameful secret you've been holding onto for decades. For others, it could mean quitting your job and chasing that dream you've kept in the back of your mind since you were a kid.

In summation, vulnerability means being honest, authentic, and real. It means allowing you to see yourself or allowing yourself to be seen by someone else.

Vulnerability is scary. It carries a lot of risks. You could show yourself to someone and be judged or rejected. You could finally go to the doctor about that problem you have and find out your health is a lot worse than you thought. You could fail at your first business venture and lose all your savings in the process.

There are a ton of risks in embracing vulnerability. But the empowerment and life that are gained in taking those risks is something beyond measure.

For me, I embrace my vulnerability by choosing to be myself, even though my authentic self was so heavily rejected in the past. I recognize I could be rejected all over again. I could also mess up the patterns I have established. But the vulnerability is worth it, because in being vulnerable, I get to be me. I've set myself free. And there is no amount of safety I would ever exchange that for.

2. Accept the Difference Between Opinions and Facts

Some people think my tattoos are hideous and childish. Some people think that I should be embarrassed by this book. Some people think I'm unattractive. Some people think I'm annoying. Some people think the way I speak is too aggressive. Some people think I never should have gotten married in the first place. Some people think I pronounce the P's in my words too hard. Some people think I should care more about my fingernails. Some people think I should've hired someone else to record my audiobook. Some people think I make bad decisions. Some people think I walk too loudly. Some people think I should've seen the divorce coming. Some people think I should let my hair be its natural color. Some people think I should go back to my ex. Some people think I should spend more money on furniture and shoes and less money on vacations. Some people think I should clean my car more regularly. Some people think I should post less personal stuff on social media.

You get the point. People have opinions about everything. Things that are small, things that are big, and things that are none of their damn business in the first place.

Everyone, from my very closest friends and family to random strangers on the internet, has opinions about me, my choices, and my life. As they will with you.

As annoying as their opinions may be, it's okay for them to have them. Because it's simply human nature for people to have thoughts and opinions. They can't stop themselves (although they could certainly be more thoughtful about how they express those thoughts and opinions). Either way, the fact is, someone will have an opinion about everything.

It doesn't matter what their opinion is. What matters is how you hold strong to your own opinions despite theirs. Do not allow yourself to be swayed and manipulated into changing who you are and how you feel about yourself, your choices, and your life so that you can try and create more positive opinions from the people around you. That's simply absurd.

And remember that just because other people feel a certain way about your choices, whether they be something small, like how you dress for work, or something big, like how many kids you decide to have and when you decide to have them, that doesn't make their thoughts true.

You get to decide what you believe and how you feel about your choices. How do you do that? Well....

3. Get to Know Yourself

Ask yourself, "Who am I?" and "Who do I want to be?"

I know, I know, these questions may seem so cheesy and cliché. How does someone answer questions like that anyways? I'm not saying you have to answer the questions eloquently or in a way that's understandable for anyone else. In fact, you don't really need to have an answer at all. The point is that you should at least ask the questions and think honestly about your responses.

One of the first steps in shedding the skin of a people pleaser is living the life that is right FOR YOU. Not for your parents, not for your doctors, not for your friends, and not for your partner.

For example, a sports doctor once told me my particular body type wasn't built to run a full marathon and I should just settle for running half marathons. I thought about how glad I was that I didn't listen to her when I crossed the finish line of my first marathon. Crossing that finish line, just a few weeks after the soul-shattering divorce from my husband, was probably the most singularly powerful and fulfilling moment of my entire life. And I wouldn't have had that moment if I took as fact this one person's opinion about who I was and what I was capable of.

As an adult, you can take in the advice, desires, and expectations of everyone around you and still decide for yourself what is best for you.

I chose the particular example of my ADHD medicine for this chapter because most of us had to become someone we weren't and do things we never wanted to do in order to survive our childhoods.

As we grow up, we generally try to keep ourselves safe, fit in, figure out who we are, and find love along the way. In pursuit of those aims, we try on a lot of different hats and often seek out various pursuits we later realize were never good for us. We get accustomed to habits, people, and ways of seeing ourselves that may actually be toxic.

People pleasers in particular get so caught up in trying to be all the right things for everyone around them, that we don't even know who we really are outside of trying to please these other people.

Maybe you spent your whole life studying to become a doctor, even though you're grossed out by the human body and are much more interested in geology. Maybe you spent your whole life hiding and running from your real sexuality. Maybe you stayed in a relationship with someone because you thought it was the right thing to do but not because you were in love. Maybe you have done things that disgust you, but you did them anyway because you feared rejection from your peers or loved ones.

There are a thousand different scenarios where we make

seemingly small choices to keep other people happy that turn into lifelong patterns of denying who we really are. We may have never approved of these patterns, but even so, they seemed like "the right thing to do." These decisions are what "kept the peace" with others and within ourselves. And now, ten years later, we are angry at ourselves for becoming this person we don't believe in or even like. Bitterly, we look in the mirror and realize we aren't living life for ourselves, but for everyone else, and it's exhausting.

One way to get to know yourself is to truly embrace alone time. Figure out, through trial and error, who you really are and who you really want to be without anyone else's feedback or opinions. Start by taking yourself out on a solo date or even better a solo vacation. Planning a vacation or finding a hobby that is entirely for you is a simple and easy way to learn who you are and what you really enjoy. Quality time with just you, doing something you think of as fun, is a great way to bond with your inner self.

4. Make a Choice

If you can think of a pattern that you embrace only to please other people that brings anxiety or turmoil to your life, consider these steps.

Step 1: Make four lists.

List A is what you **gain** from **continuing** the pattern.

For example: by continuing to quiet myself through medication, I gain consistent stability to function at high levels. I gain the appropriate behavior that people tend to find pleasing. I gain control over my impulses.

List B is what you **lose** from **continuing** the pattern.

For example: by continuing to quiet myself through medication, I lose the courage to be the loud, bold, inspired woman I long to be. I lose the pride and strength that comes from controlling my own body. I lose the possibility of a new life as a new version of myself.

List C is what you may **lose** from **discontinuing** the pattern.

For example: by choosing not to take my medicine today, I may lose the respect of the people around me, including my boss, family, and friends. I may lose the ability to easily grind through unexciting tasks. I may lose the consistency of having my emotions subdued. I may lose the ability to focus on things that don't hold my interest.

List D is what you may **gain** from **discontinuing** the pattern.

For example: by choosing not to take my medicine today, I may gain pride, self-esteem, power, and the ability to become the person I so long to be. Although I may lose my ability to focus on boring tasks, in doing so, I may gain the inspiration, courage, and desire necessary to seek out and create a life that actually excites me. I may gain a life in which I love myself much deeper than I currently do. I may gain respect for myself.

Step 2: Once you have your list, compare your options.

Step 3: I forever and always suggest that you find a safe person to speak to about how you feel and about the decisions you are considering, not because you want them to make the decision for you, but because talking with others about significant and vulnerable changes in our lives can be surprisingly empowering. Further, doing so puts the thought out into the world, thus bringing it into the light and into reality.

Step 4: Become aware that just because this is the life you lived thus far, it doesn't mean it is the life you will lead forever. You have the power and the responsibility to become who you want to be in this life.

Step 5: Make a choice based on these steps and stick with it. Refer to your list when you feel doubtful.

5. Recognize Your Worth

You will notice a theme in this book: worth. *You have worth.* You are worthy of having a good and authentic life. Your feelings matter. Your needs matter. Your desires for this one life you have matter. YOU matter.

It is hard to go against our patterns and show up for ourselves when we spent a lifetime neglecting ourselves for the sake of others. But you're freaking worth it. Recognize your worth, gosh dang it!

CHAPTER 3

I Can Save You

*I feel as though I can and must save other
people from themselves and their problems. I feel
responsible for the feelings and behaviors of others.*

Because this book is essentially a glorified therapy session we are, of course, going to go there. To the place all personal life stories go: all the way back to the parents.

I was about seven years old and excited beyond reason. I was going to my first ever Girl Scout father-daughter dance. I was never a fan of wearing dresses and typically preferred jeans, cowboy boots, and a t-shirt with a dinosaur on it. But on this day, I gladly wore the poufiest, sparkliest dress I had and danced around the living room in mental preparation.

I was excited and nervous. Not only was I going to have to dance in front of people, but this was also the first time my friends would get to meet my dad. They would all set their eyes upon the most creative, funny, dashing man they had ever seen. He would enter the room, and immediately sweep them all off their feet, and in doing so would change everything. He would no longer be a story of a man. This time, he would come to life. My prayers of what he could be would come true. People would know him, and he would be mine. My own living, breathing, real-life Dad.

Not caring about wrinkling my poufy little dress, I knelt on the couch, looked out the front window, and waited for his pickup truck to park in front of the house. The clock ticked, and I waited. And waited. And waited. As the sun began to set, I thought, *maybe he's just running late. Things happen. Right?*

As the sun left the sky, my mom came into the living room and told me he wasn't coming. My mom tried to hug me, but I brushed her off, went straight to my room, and closed the door.

Not even caring enough to take off that stupid little dress, I went to my bed and knelt in prayer. "Lord, hear my prayer. Please take care of my dad. He needs you right now. Please help him." The grip of my fingers hardened, and the tears began to fall. "Please, tell me what I'm doing wrong. Tell me what I need to do, and I'll do it. Tell me how to save him."

My father was not a consistent presence in my childhood. To his credit, he desperately wanted to drink from his own "world's best Dad" coffee cup, and live up to all that his parents had been for him. He longed to be there for me as a noble, trustworthy, great example of a man. But life hardly ever goes according to plan.

When my father was fighting withdrawal or in the stages of relapse, he put my family in dangerous and traumatic situations. To protect us, my mother had rules and strict boundaries placed on his relationship with me, her, and my brother. But at the same time, she didn't want to keep me from knowing him or keep him from knowing me. And my father took full advantage of the love and grace we shared with him.

Following every disappearance, he showed up at our front door, asking me to allow him the chance to start over. He expressed how sorry he was and that his biggest regret in life was letting me down. He said he learned from the mistakes of his past. He changed. He was a brand-new man. A man that I could trust. A man that I *should* trust.

And each time, I stood in the doorway, looking at a man with authentic ache and sorrow in his eyes. And I gave in. I caved into his sadness and his charm.

Ah yes, that charm of his could melt even the wickedest of witches. He had this strange charisma and always knew how to make a lady blush. He just had to look at me with those sad brown eyes and give me that undeniable smile, catching me in his intoxicating web of promises before saying anything at all.

Then he'd pull out the most poetic lines a girl's ever heard:

"You are the sunrise that brings light to my day."

"You are the reason I'm trying to be a better man."

"My life is not whole without you in it."

"You are the most important thing in my life."

"We need each other to make it through this."

And the most powerful statement of all, "I can't do this without you, my beautiful Jennifer Anne."

And I, the desperate-for-Daddy's-love little girl, was paralyzed with the need to believe him.

I'm not saying he was lying. I fully believe that he meant every word and that he loved me so dearly. However, as love filled as these types of claims may have seemed, ultimately, they muddied my understanding of what love was and encouraged a toxic co-dependent relationship between us.

Through his poetic lines, my father had a way of making me feel important. Not important in an uplifting and empowering way, but important in an *I'm responsible for my dad's life*, kind of way. Feeling this important forced my little undeveloped and desperate mind to believe that not only *could* I save him, but I was obligated to do so. When he said he could not make it without me, I believed him.

I believed, with all my heart, that his recovery depended on me. I believed that I really was his everything, his reason to get better, and the object that made his life whole. I believed that because I meant so much to him and because he meant so much to me, that I was responsible for his health and happiness, and he was responsible for mine.

I believed I could control him, that I could change him, and that I could save him. I believed that if I always let him back in, if I prayed hard enough, if I made him laugh, if I got the best grades, if I was filled with forgiveness, if I loved him deeply enough, if I believed in him hard enough, then this effort of mine would make him happy and healthy. Or at the very least, I believed my efforts would make him stay.

When he failed to be healthy, stable, and present, my conclusion was that my presence and my effort were not enough to save him. If I was his only reason to get better, and he wasn't getting better, then it followed that I was not enough of a reason for him to improve. If I was his everything, then even my everything was not enough. So, every time he failed to show up for me, I convinced myself that his absence was my fault. It was because I was not worth showing up for. I was not enough.

I took all of the responsibility for his well-being off him and put it on myself. Thus, not only did I feel responsible for his happiness, but I made him responsible for mine. I did not allow myself to be happy unless he was also happy. This codependent relationship was not fair to him and especially not fair to me.

As he stood in my doorway, with teary eyes, saying how sorry he was to have let me down again, promising this time would be different, I didn't think I had any option *but* to let him back in my life. Because as his angel, his heart, his sunrise, his purpose in life, and all the other titles he gave me, all he needed to get better was *me*. And I could not deprive him of myself, no matter how badly he hurt me emotionally. No matter how little I trusted him. No matter how angry I was. No matter how aware I was of the impending disappointment and heartbreak. I had to forgive him. I had to do everything I could do to save him.

And before you knew it, our relationship seemed to heal. We went to the pool, played board games, had lunch, played catch, told jokes, and even had sleepovers at his house. He serenaded me with songs he wrote for me or made me beautiful drawings. At one point, he even coached my little league soccer team. I felt like I actually had a dad, a good dad. The kind of dad he wanted to be. The kind of dad I needed him to be.

But there's this reality about patterns; they repeat.

Like a sappy drama movie, I sat waiting in the rain on the curb of the little league soccer field parking lot. The clouds poured down on me as I looked out into the now dusky sky, hoping, praying. As reality set in, my gaze dropped from the entrance of the parking lot to the defeated puddle of rainwater building around my soccer cleats.

In my soaking wet socks, waiting for a man who would not show up, I cried in prayer, asking God, "What am I doing wrong?"

My mom came to pick me up and told me, "It's not your fault. He is just a sick man who, despite how much he loves you, has problems of his own to deal with." She repeated, "It's not your fault. I'm so sorry."

But my mom's words didn't imprint in my mind the way my father's did. His words, subconsciously, said his problems and inability to show up for me *was* my fault. His words said his life revolved around me and my forgiveness of him. His words said he owned me, and I owned him. His words said we had an unbreakable bond that could not be thwarted by even the most painful of actions.

His words said that no matter how badly he fucked with my head, it was still my responsibility to love and to save him. And it was his responsibility to keep showing up at my doorstep, no matter what consequences might await his potential failings. Our lives rested in each other's hands.

I deeply internalized the idea that if my father failed, so did I. His failures weren't really his at all; they were mine. I was the reason. Maybe I didn't make him laugh enough, maybe I didn't say the right things, maybe I didn't pray hard enough. Maybe I was just too annoying or loud for him. I was so stuck inside of this delusion that I could save him, that when he wasn't "saved," it was of course my fault.

And it's not like I could talk about these feelings with anyone. How could I? How could I shine a light on my failings as a daughter?

I needed to be the savior. I needed to make people happy and keep them proud. I thought if I pointed out just how bad I was at being a daughter, they would be so disappointed, and it would just make everything even worse.

I held my thoughts and feelings all inside, allowing the negative self-talk to eat at me from the inside. I had to be brave and move forward in the face of fear and heartbreak. I had to be the good girl who got over herself, let go of her own needs, and remained loyal to those most important to her. I had to be a warrior.

Now, I know I talk a lot about feeling like I wasn't good enough as a kid and all my emotional baggage, which, while real, is not a full description of my childhood. I don't want to mislead you into thinking I had a tragic upbringing. Despite this completely unstable father-daughter relationship, the sprouting seed of self-resentment, and the pill-popping for ADHD, I was still a strong kid with a totally thriving life.

Overall, life was good. I grew up with four loving grandparents. My maternal grandmother, in particular, was my closest friend growing up. She taught me almost everything I know: how to do math without crying, how to swim and ride a bike, how to plant a seed and later eat its fruit, how to have humility and grace, how to bake a cake from scratch, how to bear-proof a campsite, how to dream bigger than society allows, and how to keep moving forward when life tries to knock you down. She affirmed my life on a daily basis and was a constant reminder of what it means to be a powerful, independent, love-filled woman.

I had one obnoxiously loving older brother who often brought himself to tears from laughing so hard at his own jokes. He entertained me for hours every day with silly pranks, mud fights in the backyard, building forts out of blankets and furniture in the living room, and scary stories at night.

My mom, who is the definition of love, was always creating new games for me to play or art projects for me to get my hands dirty. I had bunches of aunts, uncles, and cousins, all of whom brought their own sense of love and beauty into my life.

I went on road trips and airplane rides. I got out in nature, caught fireflies in jars and frogs with my bare hands. I had sleepovers and birthday parties with homemade piñatas. I rode horses and roller coasters, swam in the ocean, and climbed trees. I did my homework, acted in school plays, cuddled with my cats, and was often tucked into bed at night with a story or a song. I had sunburns, bruises, and calloused feet from a childhood well-lived.

The good in my life easily outweighed the bad. I had so many people to look to and so much going for me. Until one day, when the fun and joy I had holding me together caught fire and turned to ash around my feet. And I, no longer held together, fell apart.

When I "lost" my mom, everything stopped being doable. I should clarify, she didn't die, and I mean no disrespect to anyone who has actually lost a loved one to death. But "lost" is honestly the most appropriate word I can think of when it comes to this chapter of my life.

My mom has a zest for life, music, art, and adventure. She has an unmatchable strength, resilience, and ability to love. She shows up for the people she loves in the most authentic and inspiring ways. She fuels me when I'm running low and heals me when I'm unwell, both physically and emotionally. She has the wisdom of an aged monk and the spirit of a young child. She always believed in me and encouraged me to believe in myself. So "losing" her was one of the most difficult seasons of life I have ever been through.

Right around my first year of middle school, my family was struck by a trauma. The incident was like a lightning bolt shot from the sky, and it set our lives on fire. First, there was the lightning bolt, which was unexpected, terrifying, and painful. Then there was the fire the lightning ignited. Grief, fear, and metaphorical firefighting were our new reality.

This new reality broke my heart and utterly shattered my mother's. My mom, who already faced more trauma in her life than she knew what to do with, was confronted with a situation that even she could not bounce back from. The effects from this bolt of lightning caused my mom to spiral down the very dangerous slide of depression.

Now I am not here to discuss with you the various opinions about what depression is, how it manifests, or how to heal your way out of it. But I have seen what depression can do to a person. I've watched it take over and crush so many people that I love, myself included. The destruction can happen suddenly or slowly over time. But regardless of how depression shows up, it finds a way to suck the life right out of you. Depression creates a very real space in which people lose themselves.

Depression has the ability to take hold of a person and make the people and activities they love unimportant. It can cause people to turn into the version of themselves they promised they would never become.

In his book, *The Noonday Demon: An Atlas of Depression,* Andrew Solomon wrote, "When you are depressed, the past and future are absorbed entirely by the present moment, as in the world of a three-year-old. You cannot remember a time when you felt better, at least not clearly; and you certainly cannot imagine a future time when you will feel better."

In other words, when you are depressed, you become stuck, frozen in time and emotion. Your life seems to lose its future and becomes a purgatory from which you cannot escape.

This cycle of despair was the case for my mother. Her body physically came home from work every day, but her mind, her soul, and her spark that once lit our house with love and laughter did not follow. She seemed lost in a thick fog of grief and terror. She was present, but not really. Like a shadow of herself. Depression cast a blanket of fear, sadness, and emptiness throughout the house.

I, of course, did not just watch from the sidelines. I fought the fire right alongside her and was devastated by the way it burned her.

I took all her sadness, all her fear, all her darkness and placed it on my list of things that needed fixing. I felt responsible for every tear. I tried with all my might to get her out of bed, to cheer her up, and make her see the world more clearly, with its green grass and blue skies. I wanted her to see herself for the phenomenal independent woman I knew her to be. Sometimes my efforts worked, and she cheered up long enough to eat dinner or watch a movie with me. In these glimpses of consciousness, she told me, "You are so amazing, I don't think I could make it without you."

In her mind, her comment meant, *I love you, thank you for being here with me.* But in my mind, it meant, *I need you to save me.*

And when, despite my truest, deepest efforts, I could not save her, I felt like a complete failure. Watching this fire burn down my life and the scars it left on my mother's skin filled the portfolio of my most painful memories. Especially since the trauma that caused her depression spiral was something I had to process too.

I still had friends. I still went to school. I still had a life. But none of that mattered at the end of the day when I came home to a house that was empty and cold. I had no one to count on anymore besides myself.

I felt responsible for saving my entire family. For years my dad was gone, God-knows-where; my brother was a masterful, heartbreaking wreck; and my mom was technically there, but she wasn't really there at all.

I was just a little kid, trying with all the energy I had in me to fix everything and everyone, to save everyone from their own demons, to cure their addictions, to curb their anger, to stifle their self-harm, to prevent them from hurting each other, and to encourage their self-care. I was holding all of them in my arms while I was still in pieces on the floor.

What little self-love I had remaining was buried under an increasing pile of anger, bitterness, and self-resentment. I was angry at God, angry at the world, and so fucking angry at myself. I tried to save them. I was supposed to save them. It's why I was born. (Or so I thought). But I just couldn't do it. I just wasn't good enough to heal them. That little sprouting seed of self-resentment began to blossom into an intense mental and physical hatred of self.

During this time, my people pleasing escalated from moderate to extreme. I did not receive the affection, attention, and presence from my people that I so desperately needed. I felt in order to get the love I needed, I had to bend over backward to fix everyone else. From this point on, my concept of my self-worth was fully wrapped in my ability to save other people, which I was unable to do. So, in turn, I felt completely worthless.

And sadly, when a person feels worthless, they don't treat themselves very well. To cope with the anger and the lack of control, I took control in the places where I could claim it. I constantly redecorated my room, I started running, I wrote poetry, I made art, and I studied hard. But when none of those activities satisfied, the self-hatred manifested into a desire to hurt myself.

Any time I faced feelings of overwhelm, fear, or pain, I found a secluded space and physically and emotionally attacked myself.

I often stood in front of the mirror and contorted my vision of myself through a lens of complete and utter disgust. I hit myself, choked myself, scratched myself, banged my head against the wall, carved into my skin, punched things until my hands bled, and bit the inside of my mouth until I tasted blood. I let people treat me however they wanted and wished for terrible things to happen to me. I prayed for death.

None of the self-harm made me feel better though. It all made me feel much worse. I was a smart kid, and I knew better than to act in such a harmful way. And when I finished hurting myself or giving parts of myself away to the people in my life, I was filled to the brim with shame. I knew I deserved better from myself and the people around me. But I had so many emotions I couldn't deal with, so much pent-up energy and aggression inside of me that I just exploded in these moments of physical and mental self-hatred.

I wasn't like some crazy, self-abusive kid all the time, especially out in public. I never talked to anyone about how I treated myself or how I felt. My best friend had small glimpses into my world and my head, but even then, there was only so much she could do and only so much I told her. I never allowed myself to talk to anyone about how I truly felt because I didn't want to look like a failure. I still tried to be the savior. I still tried to make everyone happy and proud. I still tried to be the "good girl."

Today, as an emotionally and mentally thriving adult, I look back on these moments and can easily feel sad and sorry for that little girl. I wish that I could go back and talk some sense into her and give her a self-love hug. I wish that I could go back in time and change what happened.

I have no doubt that both of my parents feel the same way. I know that if they could go back and change the past, they would. In fact, reading all of this in a published book is probably deeply painful and embarrassing for them. And for that, I am truly sorry.

But I am not sorry enough to not write this chapter, because I know for a fact, I was not the only little kid out there who had a hard time learning to love themselves because they felt responsible for their very human families. I know I'm not the only person who turned on themselves because they couldn't save the people they loved. I know I am not the only one still trying to heal from the trauma of my childhood. And we people pleasers all have childhood baggage, usually riddled with some level of parental neglect, or else we would already know how to properly love ourselves.

I also am not sorry for writing this chapter because this is my real story. Lying to ourselves and sugar coating what really happened in our lives is counterproductive. To grow from our stories, we have to face our truths, no matter how embarrassing or difficult they may be to look at or to share with others. My parents had to face their truths and I had to face my own.

While we all wish we could go back to change what happened in the past, the simple truth is we can't. The only thing we can do is process what we went through or what we did or didn't do and use those experiences to make ourselves better people in the current moment. This task requires self-forgiveness, which I discuss thoroughly in Chapter 6.

While I describe a lot of my personal business in this book, I realize this chapter shares other people's stories outside of my own. Let me be clear: this chapter is not intended to shame my parents for their seasons of unwellness. This chapter isn't a way to place blame on my parents for my own problems. And this chapter is not a pity party to create some sort of illusion that I had a "hard life."

So why did I write this chapter? Well, I'm glad you asked.

This chapter chronicles my most profound experiences of punishing myself for other people's actions. This chapter shares where my hero complex and codependent attitude towards all of my relationships originated. This chapter shows how people pleasers can mistake a lack of control as a lack of love, importance, or self-worth.

I grew up with the idea that I could control others by loving them deeply enough, being on my best behavior, and helping them through their struggles. This belief that I *could* change the behaviors of others encouraged me to blame myself when other people failed to change.

I became emotionally violent and physically abusive towards myself when other people didn't act as I wanted or needed them to. I allowed the actions and words of other people to determine how I felt about myself and how I treated myself.

Lastly, I allowed my disapproval of other people's behavior to create resentment in place of authentic compassion and love.

My childhood was weighed down by unattainable, or at least uncontrollable standards that I set for myself.

My first standard was that everyone I knew and loved should be happy and healthy. Off the bat, this rule is clearly something no twelve-year-old kid, or any human being for that matter, could possibly control.

Further, "happy" and "healthy" are both subjective terms that have different meanings for different people. So, you could translate this standard to say: "Everyone I know is living their life in line with my expectations." This standard sounds less flattering than the original sentence but is a far more accurate description of what I actually felt and thought.

I expected my father would show up for me every time he promised he would. I expected to wake up one day and suddenly have my mom back. I expected my brother's healing to stay consistent. And when these standards I held for others weren't met, I took it as a failing on my part.

The second standard was that I should feel happy and strong at all times. To validate my sense of self-worth I felt I had to be all things for everyone. I had to be everyone's source of inspiration, joy, and peace. I had to be their strength when they were feeling weak. I had to be their spine when they were feeling shaky. I had to be their smile when they were feeling sad. I had to be their reasoning when they weren't thinking clearly. And in order to sustain that level of giving, I had to be happy and strong all the time. I had to be consistent.

These are some very unforgiving expectations to live up to. I corrupted my mind to believe that because these standards were not consistently met in my life, there must be something wrong with me. I must be doing life all wrong.

When I didn't feel happy or strong, I felt ashamed. When my family didn't live up to my expectations, I felt ashamed. When the people around me suffered, I felt ashamed. Shame was my constant companion.

All of these standards followed me into my adult life. They caused tension and self-sabotage in my romantic relationships, my friendships, and my familial relationships. Whether someone had depression, a bad attitude, unhealthy eating habits, fits of anger or sadness, various addictions, work problems, or trouble with the law, I saw these behaviors as a threat to our collective "health and happiness."

I felt a constant, overwhelming, and uncontrollable urge to "save" people from themselves. In other words, I tried to change everyone around me "for their own good." And worst of all, I resented them for not caring about our collective "health and happiness" enough to change themselves.

This pattern was especially true in my romantic relationships. When my partners failed to show up for themselves in the ways I wanted them to, I felt unimportant. And when they failed to show up for me and the relationship in the ways I expected them to, I blamed myself. I kept thinking I just wasn't enough.

If they didn't fit in with my definition of what "happy and healthy" looked like, then I concluded that my happiness was not important to them. I must not be important to them. I must be unworthy.

My mind read the situation as, *they smoke cigarettes, therefore there must be something wrong with me. I must not be reason enough for them to change.* In my mind, I regressed into the little girl waiting in the rain for her dad to pick her up from soccer practice, believing that she was just not worth showing up for.

And, my dear readers, while on the surface, my desire for others to be healthy and to show up for themselves (and me) may seem like positive energy, in reality, the way I reacted when those standards weren't met was filled with anything but love.

I made everything all about me, even when it was a whole different person who had the problems. If someone I cared about experienced sadness, anger, addiction, health problems or anything negative, I made their suffering all about me and how their behavior, actions, and emotions made me feel.

Trying to "fix" my loved ones was never 100% about love. While my reaction to their pain may have been birthed from a place of love, it manifested into a desire to control others, so they fit better into what I wanted and perhaps needed them to be. My response was more about me than it was about them.

When you fixate on your ideal of who other people *should* be and how they *should* act, it becomes increasingly easy to resent them for not fitting into this mold you have made for them. When you are unable to accept people for who or where or what they are, any "help" you offer, while presented as an act of love, is more deeply an act of control to help you manage your own ego.

To love ourselves well, we need to be able to see ourselves and other people as completely separate. Even if you share blood, even if you share a bed, even if you share a kid, you are not responsible for or in control of someone else's behavior or emotions. Nor are they responsible for or in control of yours.

To an extent, we all have a responsibility to support and show up for the people we love. But there is a line, and it is thin. Once "showing up" turns into blame, shame, resentment, and especially hate, you've crossed the line. Once you allow other people's actions to determine how you feel, especially how you feel about yourself, you've crossed the line.

Blaming anyone but my dad for my dad's issues was misguided. Carrying the pain of my family while they suffered and ignoring my hurt was counterproductive. Hating myself because my mom was depressed, was not love. Blaming God for my inability to change other people was simply incorrect.

Learning where those lines lie has been one of the most difficult and transformative processes of my adult life. Detaching myself from others and detaching others from me was the closest action to "setting myself free" that I have ever known.

Had I not unlearned these patterns, they could have turned even darker. Adults who maintain a hero complex or codependent behaviors very slowly eat away at their mental health. These behaviors can manifest into very real psychological disorders, like anxiety or depression, both of which I have experienced. And let me tell you now, they both absolutely suck.

Codependency can erode your control over your emotions, your ability to set boundaries, and your capacity to communicate authentically. You can become obsessed with pleasing others and lose all sense of self-worth and self-esteem. Who you are can become wrapped up in how other people act and feel. You also can enable other people's bad behavior because you want to keep them "happy."

Further, codependency can create a space in which you feel so completely out of control of your own life that you fall into self-destruction, just to feel in control. Self-mutilation and self-harm are most often manifestations of your inability to ask for help. In the words of Lady Gaga, "I was a cutter for a long time, and the only way that I was able to stop cutting and self-harming myself was to realize that what I was doing was trying to show people that I was in pain instead of telling them and asking for help."

Personally, I was so concerned about upsetting people that I refused to tell anyone how miserable and overwhelmed I really was. I was afraid to be honest in the fear of hurting their feelings. I was unable to show up for myself at all because I was so consumed with saving everyone else. I didn't want to be anyone's burden.

I'm not saying the answer to this issue is to be so obsessed with yourself that you don't show up for the people you love. You should be there for the people you love. But "being there" and "loving" someone does not mean taking responsibility for their problems, on any level.

Acts of Self-Love to Practice

1. Speak Up

Inside of every last one of us exists an inner child. And that inner child is exactly what it sounds like. Deep inside, we ALL are just little kids in need of protection, acceptance, and love. Protect your inner child from the emotional abuse of others. If someone is hurting you emotionally, tell them. Stand up for yourself.

As actual children, we don't have the mental capacities to truly stick up for ourselves. But once we become adults, we absolutely have every responsibility to protect and be there for that little kid. And sometimes, all that means is telling someone, "I love you, but the way you are treating me hurts. And something here needs to change."

During my childhood, I never told anyone how angry I was. I never said anything that could hurt someone's feelings or make them uncomfortable. I specifically didn't speak up to the people who caused me pain because I wanted to heal them, not make the problem worse.

I thought keeping my feelings inside was an act of being strong for them. I thought allowing others to decide my boundaries for me was love. I thought I was doing the right thing. I just wanted to be "good." But the reality is, I neglected myself and resented them in the process. I was waiting for someone else to come and save me, but now I know I need to step up and save myself.

Full lists of resources are available on this very topic, specifically when it comes to women in abusive relationships. Not every situation is that extreme, however. Sometimes it's just someone relying too heavily on you for their own sanity or health. Both situations matter. And in situations like this, the greatest act of self-love you can practice is just speaking up.

2. Stop Trying to Change People

The honest truth is you can't change others. People are not puppets. People don't change because of you. People change because of themselves.

I do not believe there is such a thing as good or bad people. In my belief system, there are simply good or bad choices, and choices can change, thus people can change. But you cannot change someone else's choices. No matter how badly we wish we could just make other people's choices for them, we cannot.

There is this weird pattern where people-pleasers are drawn to unstable people because we like the idea of being able to heal them. And while being there for your people is such a beautiful thing, thinking that you are somehow "saving" them from themselves is not really love, it's an ego trip.

We people pleasers can easily mistake control for love.

But love does not require control. Allow people the freedom to make their own mistakes. Allow people the freedom to make their own choices.

I'm not saying that you should accept poor treatment from others. But I am saying, if someone else is treating you or themselves poorly, you must come to terms with the fact that you are not going to change them. If a person in your life is unable to meet your needs and be there for you in the ways you need, that is something you have to accept. It is not something you can manipulate into being different.

You are not responsible for changing other people's behavior. However, you are responsible for protecting your inner child. You are responsible for yourself, your choices, and your life.

Your needs matter too. Focus on changing you. Cause at the end of the day, that's where your real power lies.

3. Forgive Those Who Failed You

What even is forgiveness? There are a thousand different definitions and thoughts on what forgiveness is. Here's mine: forgiveness is letting go. Point blank.

Anger, resentment, bitterness, regret, and various other emotions are important. They exist in your body and mind for a reason. They are there to protect you from being hurt again. So, it is very natural to want to hold on to them and keep them close, to quilt a blanket out of them and wrap yourself in it, so no one can ever hurt you again.

Instead, I suggest that you feel the anger. Feel the bitterness. Write them down. Pray about them. Scream them into the lyrics of an angry punk song. Talk about these feelings with a therapist, with the person you are angry with, with yourself, and with your God. Allow the feelings to exist, recognize why they are there, thank them for showing up for you, and then let them the fuck go.

I could easily bust into a Frozen song here, but for the sake of us all, I will not.

Let it go y'all. Breathe in love and breathe out that toxic bullshit you have been holding on to for your whole life.

I, of all people, can tell you practicing the art of letting things go is something that takes time, patience, and consistency. Little by little, step by step, and breath by breath, let it in, then let it out.

Honestly, just go talk to a therapist, because forgiveness is super freaking hard to figure out and often requires professional help.

4. Don't Get Lost in Your Love

This chapter is written from the perspective of a daughter, sister, friend, and partner. However, I cannot speak from the perspective of a parent.

I don't have kids, so I can't truly relate to the pressures and instinctual desires to protect and raise children to be all that you ever hoped they could be and none of what you hoped they wouldn't be. I have not experienced the deep guilt and pain felt when your child faces struggles you hoped they would never have to go through. I don't know what it's like to be responsible for the upbringing of a whole entire person, and then for that person to get sick, be hurt, or have to suffer the consequences of self-destructive choices.

I don't know the feeling of dedicating your life to creating opportunities for someone else, and how terrible the lack of control must feel when that person falls off the path you so carefully cultivated for them, whether it be by their own hand or that of fate.

But I can imagine that when I eventually help raise little humans, I will feel guilty when they fall. I will feel the need to sacrifice myself to make proper space for their growth. I will fall into moments of disappointment and despair when they call me to say they messed up again. I will hurt when they hurt. I will cry when they cry. I will feel what they feel. The love I have for them will feel all consuming.

However, I also imagine, I will do everything within my power to not lose myself or my sense of self-worth amid all the emotions, connection, and desperation that come with being a parent. I will remember that even though I am responsible for this little life, I will not allow my life to be lost within the pressures or mistakes of that important and heavy load. And when I'm feeling that overwhelming need to save them, I will remind myself that they are not a branch of my body that I can bend to my will, but rather an entirely separate person all their own. While we will share in each other's pain, we are our own beings, living separate lives.

Maybe I can't exactly relate to being a parent, but I can imagine that at the end of the day, it's still just love. And maybe, "I'm not a smart man, but I know what love is."

While love, especially parental love, is one of the most overwhelming and powerful forces humans get to experience, it is not the entirety of who we are or our reason for existing. At least not according to this book. To me, love is simply a part of the whole and we can (and must) learn to embrace it in ways that lift us and fill our cups instead of allowing it to drown and consume us.

This same idea falls into smaller day-to-day emotions as well. When I see someone I love looking upset, I compulsively feel responsible for comforting them and trying to cheer them up. And again, while it is kind and healthy to show up for our people, we need to make sure we are doing so without crossing our boundaries and allowing ourselves to be brought down into their despair, hurt, or loss.

CHAPTER 4

I Need You

I am dependent on my relationships with others to validate my sense of self-worth. This causes me to stress over the needs of others while fully neglecting my own and keeps me from being able to leave relationships even when they've become unhealthy. This pattern is commonly associated as a symptom of an "anxious attachment style."

In Chapter 2, I briefly introduced you to "the pit." The pit refers to the void or feeling of emptiness that is created within you when your sense of self-worth is not reinforced by holistic and authentic self-love.

As a young child, I had immense love for myself. I saw the light inside of me and expressed it in all the ways my heart wanted to. However, as I got older and experienced continual rejection, abandonment, inconsistent parenting, and, you know, just general life, I began to fight against my light and replaced my self-love with feelings of shame, inadequacy, self-loathing, and desperation.

The love I had for myself was no longer unconditional. My love for myself had to be earned through other people's presence, approval, and attention.

But the pit can't be filled by anything other than authentic and unconditional *self-love*. So, no matter how much presence, approval, and attention I received from the people around me, I still felt empty inside. These seemingly fulfilling acts from others just brought momentary highs.

I became desperate to fill my emptiness with all the people I came into contact with, including my romantic relationships, my friendships, my relationships with family members, and in my professional career.

This belief laid out a welcome mat for manipulative and emotionally harmful people to enter and set up camp in my life. I constantly ignored and forgave unhealthy treatment from others in order to maintain them as a source of "fulfillment" in my life. I became overly attached to anyone who made me feel momentarily seen and wanted, and I refused to let them go, even when they clearly did more harm than good to my emotional state.

When I first entered the world of dating, I basically handed myself over to interested persons. If they wanted me to dress, talk, or act a certain way, I obliged.

My first romantic relationship was no exception. I didn't even like him. In fact, I barely even knew him. All the interactions we had were purely physical with no real connection involved.

I was ashamed of this because I wanted to be loving with someone out of love, and not out of loneliness, as was the case. But, at the same time, he made me feel seen and he gave me moments of fullness. And I wanted more of that not-so-alone-and-empty feeling. So, I went back to him.

I told him that I loved him, even though I didn't. I smiled when he said, "I love you too," even though we both knew he didn't. I told him what we were doing was okay, even though I didn't really feel okay about it at all.

But even though I knew how fake and insincere the "relationship" was, I still wanted him. Or, at least, I wanted him to want me. I had awareness but lacked the self-love to acknowledge what my actual needs were. Even amidst a hurricane of visibly rotting fruit and poisoned apples, I still dreamt of an everlasting feast. I still drew his name in my notebook. I still wanted a promise of always. I still fantasized about him sweeping me in his arms and carrying me away to a better, not-so-empty place.

I was so empty of self-love that I wished a man I didn't even like would stay, and I willingly gave away my dignity and self-respect in attempts to make a relationship with him happen.

When I was unable to fill the void inside of me with authentic love for myself, then being alone without anyone to temporarily fill me meant feeling empty and loveless. This fear of the impending, loveless abyss made me wildly desperate. This desperation made me attach to anyone, even if they were not healthy for me. It made me seek to please anyone who would let me.

In the case of my first romantic relationship, this fear caused me to cross my boundaries. I put myself in uncomfortable, and quite honestly dangerous situations, just to try and please this guy. And even though I felt awful after every one of our encounters, I still held on and went back for more. That fear of the abyss lingered in the back of my head and refused to let me let him go.

It wasn't until I met the next guy that I was able to let the first one go. And consecutively, throughout my life, I have not been able to let go of any romantic partner until I was fully invested in someone else. I was unable to be alone. I was terrified by the idea of being attached to no one. The fear and pain of not having someone else's love and attention to validate my worth far outweighed the pain and fear of being with someone who wasn't right for me.

That is until I divorced my husband.

Let me just start by saying, to this day I truly and authentically love my ex-husband with all my bleeding heart. He was my very best friend. He was my lighthouse in the fog, my mood stabilizer, my source of laughter, fun, and safety in what often feels like such a dangerous and complicated world.

I still hear his laugh in my head on a regular basis and I can't help but smile at the sound. He is interesting, funny, smart, creative, hardworking, and so strong and kind that back in high school he carried a full-length couch on his back for an entire mile just to make my mom smile. He's tall, talented, generous, an artist, a great conversationalist, a thoughtful gift giver, and the sickest road-trip DJ.

There were times when the light hit his face and his chest just right and he glowed. It was like the light inside of him was simply escaping through his pores. I loved the way the tight curls of his hair felt in my hands and sometimes even his smell was enough to get me high. Talking with him was as effortless as breathing. He's a straight dime on nearly every level and is hands-down the coolest person I've ever met.

The first time I brought him home to meet my mom they bonded over her record collection and then proceeded to dance around the living room to shared music taste. It was a beautiful moment. Our time together was filled with countless beautiful moments.

I was madly in love with him and had every last intention of standing by him until the day one of us died.

However, this undeniable friendship and authentic attachment to each other did not by any means translate into a perfect or even healthy relationship.

My relationship with my ex-husband was (and is) a fluid one. Since we first started dating as teenagers, our relationship has been in a constant state of fluctuation between thriving and completely unstable. There were times of unmistakable joy, steady contentment, deep connection, fiery romance, and honest intention for stability and growth. However, there were also times of painful inconsistency, careless neglect, untold truths, unbalanced power, and manipulative control over each other. This unending game of tug of war between these two versions of us was nauseating at best, and heartbreaking at worst.

But no matter how bad things got between us, I knew in the bottom of my soul that we could work through absolutely anything. Even when we both had nightmares every night. Even when we both accepted numbness to avoid the extent of our authentic pain. Even when we held on just to honor our vow, and not because we received anything good from the relationship anymore. We held on because that's what you do. Especially once you get married.

Being his wife was about more than just being married to an incredible, albeit unpredictable, man. It was also about just being a wife in general. I wasn't just holding on to his love, but also to the identity his love gave me. I became so attached to the identity of the "devoted wife" that I refused to admit defeat, even when it glared me in the face.

Being a people pleaser, the thought of divorce screamed "failure." To me, getting divorced meant I failed at being a wife. It meant I failed at achieving what I considered to be the most important goal in my life, which was to have a healthy and thriving marriage.

How could I go to my family, his family, or worst of all, face my God in prayer and tell them that we failed? That *I* failed? So many people loved us and believed in us. Our wedding was the only time I had nearly every single person I loved all in one room, and it was to celebrate and bask in the glow of our love. Everyone came to that wedding believing we would be the ones to make it. All the speeches people gave, all the hope everyone had for us filled the room with the sense that we really did something right. Our families merged together that day in such a powerful way. How could we tear that apart?

How could I, the devoted wife, end my marriage? How could I destroy the identity I had worked so hard to cultivate? How could I go from happily married wife to divorcée? I just couldn't. I dared not even think it. Divorce was simply not an option.

And in holding this belief, I allowed the heartache to build and build. I allowed our relationship to get so much worse than it needed to because I simply refused to admit defeat. I was fully invested in my ego and in this made-up identity of who I thought I was supposed to be, rather than being invested in my true self or my husband's true self.

My devotion to my husband was rooted in more than my authentic and deep love for him. It was also rooted in a need to be validated. Being his wife proved to me that I was worthy. My marriage gave me an identity that I so desperately craved and clung to.

People pleasers are desperate for validation above all else. And what higher form of validation is there than to have someone you genuinely care about tell you, "You're so fucking awesome that I vow to stand by you, until the day we die?" And what greater loss of validation is there than when that promise goes unfulfilled?

After months of marriage counseling, dozens of deeply heartbreaking conversations, a short separation, repeated disappointment, and long periods of patience and pushing my needs aside to focus on his needs, our relationship eventually reached an unthinkable peak of disrespect and emotional pain that I could simply not excuse without losing myself completely. Lines were crossed, and bridges were burned.

Once I came to grips with this reality, it hit me like a punch to the face. If I chose to stay, it would be for all the wrong reasons. At that point, staying in the marriage meant crossing my boundaries of what was acceptable and what wasn't in order to hold on to someone who was no longer healthy for me.

Leaving my husband required a detachment from my ego and a detachment from my wife identity. It required me to validate my own worth. Leaving required a complete and total rewrite of who I thought I was and where my value as a human being came from.

I spent the previous years working on my personal development and figuring out how to love myself. This self-maintenance and consistent energy towards filling in my own pit gave me the strength to walk away. When I divorced my husband, I took the stand that the little girl I used to be didn't have the courage to take.

However, that doesn't mean the loss or emptiness that came with our separation wasn't outrageously awful. For many months after our split, I felt dead inside. It was like my soul had been ripped straight out of my body. I felt like an empty shell and my life seemed utterly meaningless.

I spiraled into a very serious depression and had extreme difficulty waking up in the morning because I didn't want to face the emptiness of my bed, my home, and my life. I had an insatiable desire to fill the now-screaming void with any man I could get my hands on, alcohol, drugs, unhealthy food, 24-hour naps, and suicide.

It took all the self-love I had in me (along with the outside help of friends, family, doctors, therapists, and God) to not dive head-first into all these seemingly quick fixes for the pain.

The hardest quick fix to resist, however, was pretending nothing had happened and going back to the relationship. It was almost impossible not to run right back into his open, warm, chiseled arms. I mean this in both the metaphorical and physical sense, as being held in his arms in our nightly cuddle was one of the feelings I missed more than words can say. There had been a time when being in his arms was the safest place in the world to be. And then, all of a sudden, nowhere felt safe anymore. All the danger and chaos of the world I used him to shield me from was now bright and unavoidable.

Sleeping became my only solace. Except not really. My nightmares were so consistent and so vividly painful that being asleep was worse than being awake. But depression is a twisted beast and when I felt myself starting to wake up, I refused to allow the light to reach me. I slept for days on end, wishing to just fade away into the moments of darkness between the nightmares.

When I was awake, I thought of nothing but him. Sometimes while thinking about him, I got sucked into the good memories. I thought about all the fun he brought to my life over the years. I thought about all the laughter and joy we shared in between the dysfunction and instability.

I thought about all that he was to me. Over our nine-year relationship, my attachment to him became rock-solid, and I became heavily dependent on him to give my life meaning. I truly came to see myself as his other half and saw him as the ground beneath my feet. He was what kept me standing. So, when I officially called our marriage quits, it felt like the entire world had been pulled out from beneath me and left me falling into an abyss of emptiness.

I didn't know who I was without him. After nearly a decade together, our lives were so intertwined that pulling them apart felt impossible. It felt like death. It felt like a loss of something so much greater than love. It was a loss of me, or at least a loss of who I thought I was.

There were times when chasing vices was almost an instinctual and unavoidable reaction to my pain, like flinching when someone swings at your face. But with time, patience, and the help of the people in my life, I began to face all my feelings. I started to see the emptiness for what it was: an end, but not *the* end. It was not something I needed to, or even could, run from. Nor was this ending something I could hide behind endless amounts of queso, bottomless mimosas, or Tinder dates.

This emptiness and all the discomfort that came from being engulfed in it was something I had to feel and accept. But in facing it all, something new happened. Something I had never experienced before. Somewhere in all that hurt, somewhere in all the emptiness, I found a new me. I found a version of me that wasn't wrapped up in someone else but was instead cradled in my own arms. I found myself standing on my own ground and holding myself up. For the first time in my life, I had self-love to fill in the void.

When I fell into deep moments of despair and self-loathing, I was often blinded by the depth of the pain and the emptiness my husband's absence left in my life. But the more I began to face my demons, instead of running from them, the more I appreciated that the love I had for me ran deeper than the grief I had from losing him.

Every day I had to make a choice. Do I choose to go back to a relationship I knew was killing me, or do I choose to love myself and let it go? Do I choose to sleep all day so I can avoid my reality, or do I wake up and do the work to heal and move forward? Do I choose to distract myself with other men, or do I choose to figure out who I am outside of being someone else's person?

I choose love. Every day, as I continue to wade through the thick and suffocating waters of grief, loss, and loneliness, I continue to choose love. Even when the void in me creeps up. Even when that old, people-pleasing demon whispers in my ear to find the validation I crave in any man who will give it, I have to choose love.

Through this self-love I was able to reach for healthy substitutes for the high the relationship had once given me, like my friends, my family, writing, nature, yoga, art, journaling, and adventure. I was able to see clearly, for the first time in my entire life, that I did not need a particular person by my side for my life to have meaning or for me to feel like a whole human. I didn't need anyone's validation of my worth but my own. I didn't need a man telling me he loved me for me to know I was worthy of and already filled with love.

I'm not about to say that I don't need anyone, because that is false. I still rely heavily on others to get me through the divorce and its aftershocks. But the idea that I only needed one person to get through it all switched from needing my ex-husband to needing me. I needed to be there for myself more than ever before, especially during the very dark moments when my mind drifted to and fixated on suicidal ideation. I had to find the strength within me to pull myself out or at least to reach out a hand for someone else to pull me out of these twisted mental states.

I had to step out of my emotions and out of my body to turn around and see the ten-year-old little girl inside me, curled up in the fetal position feeling hopeless, rejected, unloved, abandoned, and used. I had to reach inside myself and wipe away her tears. I had to hold her and tell her that she still mattered. She still had value. She was just as whole as she had ever been. And then I'd grab her hand, pull her off the floor, force her to take a shower, eat something, pet her dog, pull on her running shoes, step out the door, and remember who she was. She was not anybody else's anything. She was simply Jennifer. And she would be okay without this (or any) man's love.

Learning how to disconnect from our attachments to others is wildly complicated and painful. Especially when you have an insecure attachment style like I do.

If you do not know what your attachment style is I highly recommend you find out. A quick google search will help you determine what your attachment style is.

These styles refer to how a person learned to interact with their caregivers during their very early childhood. This subconscious understanding of how relationships work is carried from childhood into adulthood.

From what we currently know, there are four main attachment styles: secure, anxious, avoidant, and disorganized. My propensity to get so attached to the validation received through my relationships categorizes me within the "anxious attachment style."

The attachment style you form is based nearly 100% on the relationship you had with your caregivers in your young childhood. For the anxiously attached, during childhood, our caregivers were typically inconsistent with their love, attention, or security, thus leaving us to believe all relationships will require extreme work on our part to keep the other person engaged, present, and actively involved in our life.

We have a desperate desire for intimacy that we constantly fear will not be reciprocated. We fear our partners will abandon us, and we become overly attached to them to compensate for this fear.

We are highly sensitive to the emotions of our partners and make attempts to regulate their emotions for them to ensure their continued presence and attention in our life. We also find it very difficult to leave a relationship, no matter how unhealthy it is, because once we attach to someone, our greatest fear becomes the loss of that attachment. We are, in essence, extremely clingy.

An anxious attachment style also encourages us to do whatever is necessary to maintain connection with our partners, including manipulating them and changing our behavior to try and get attention. More extreme cases often include obsessive jealousy.

In my case, during our nearly ten years together, I became acutely aware of my partner's needs. I was always highly conscious of his emotions. I was also highly reactive to his emotions. Even when I was at my healthiest mentally, if he got angry with me, my inner child freaked out and sent me into instinctual panic mode. I completely fell to pieces, unable to think correctly, speak, and sometimes even breathe. These intense reactions to his negative emotions were a combination of unintentional manipulation and sheer uncontrollable panic.

However, the opposite was also true. When he was really happy with me, I felt high. And I sought that high above all other things in my life. Making him happy became my top priority.

Unfortunately, this strong dedication to fulfilling his needs meant pushing my needs and happiness aside. Not to say that I was unhappy; it's simply that my happiness did not matter to me as much as his happiness. Or, in other words, his happiness was my happiness.

My partner was at times competent in fulfilling my needs and reciprocating the love and affection I shared with him, but his willingness to do so was painfully inconsistent due to his own screwed up attachment style. The irony is that I grew up learning this inconsistency was normal and to be expected, so having it play out in my adult relationships only further encouraged my anxious attachment mindset. Thus, the cycle kept repeating.

So how does one break this vicious cycle? You must start by looking at yourself. Here are a few questions to consider:

- How does this relationship serve *me*?
- Are *my* needs being met?
- Do I verbally articulate my needs to my partner? If not, why?
- Do I even know what my needs are?
- Am I able to maintain a sense of calm even when my partner is upset?

- Am I able to give my partner freedom to explore their life outside of just spending time with me?
- Do I suffer anxiety when my partner is not paying attention to me?
- Do I rely on my partner to regulate my emotions?
- Do I feel like I might die if I lose this relationship?
- Is this relationship my only source of happiness?

Think critically about your answers to these questions.

I am not suggesting that we shouldn't make sacrifices for our relationships or that we don't care about the needs and emotions of our loved ones. What I am advocating is that we also care about *our own* needs and *our own* emotions. Our happiness matters too.

The way out of the vicious cycle is to start caring about your needs. It is to put yourself first. Because as ultramarathon runner David Goggins said in his book, *Can't Hurt Me,* "No one is coming to save you." It's not that people don't want to save you or that people don't love you, but if you don't look out for you, then who is going to?

The truth is you cannot save yourself with someone else's love. Those are only temporary highs that will fade. What matters, both in your relationship with yourself and in your relationships with others, is the love you have for yourself.

No one will make your decisions but you. You are the one who has to save yourself. You are the one who must reach out for help. You are the one who has to stand up and reclaim your life. You are the love you've been waiting for. You are the hero you need. You are not waiting for the right person to come along and give your life meaning. You are waiting on you.

Over the past months, I've talked with various people going through similar heartbreaks as myself, and my statement to them all is the same: "They couldn't love you because they didn't love themselves. You have to break this cycle. You have to love yourself. In doing so the right people will gravitate toward you and you will be ready to cultivate healthy relationships. But you cannot have healthy relationships until you first learn to love yourself with or without them."

If the absence of self-love is a pit, then the presence of self-love is the soil that fills it. It is in this soil that other relationships, projects, and life experiences can grow and be fully experienced in a healthy way. As RuPaul says, "If you can't love yourself, how in the hell are you gonna love somebody else?" There is serious truth to this question. Without the soil, nothing you plant will live for very long.

But if you have well-tended soil, anything can grow. Having healthy soil means that even if a flower dies and you have to uproot it, something new can grow in its place. But if you keep your soil filled with diseased plants and no sunlight, or worse have no soil at all, then nothing else will be able to grow. You'll throw in seeds and plants and water which will feel good for a minute. But none of it will grow.

If you want your garden to grow, you have to lay the foundation, pulling out and tossing away those connections that have come to their end. You have to start by taking care of your base. You have to start by taking care of yourself.

Acts of Self-Love to Practice

1. Allow Yourself to Feel ALL of the Emotions

During the process of my divorce, I felt and often still feel all the stages of grief: denial, anger, bargaining, depression, and acceptance. I had bargaining and depression down to a science. But anger— anger was a whole other beast that I couldn't even look in the eye.

I will say it outright: people pleasers do not know how to manage or appropriately express the emotion of anger.

Once the divorce was in process, I felt enraged. But I did not express any of that anger to my ex. I just bottled it up in attempts to be kind and loving towards him during the process. I just didn't want to make things harder than they had to be. Even in our darkest hours, I still felt a deep responsibility to please him in any way I could.

Anger is just so icky to me. I'd rather sweep it under the rug and pretend it never existed.

Whenever I felt angry, I replaced that anger with patience, forgiveness, and empathy. These are all mature reactions to difficult situations. However, anger, in its proper place, is also a mature reaction, no matter how dangerous society tries to tell us anger is.

Anger protects you. Anger makes sure that you are treated fairly and decently. Anger is the friend telling you that you are worth so much more than you give yourself credit for. Anger is the guy who sticks up for you when other people don't do right by you. Anger has its place in your life, and you have to make room to express it.

I didn't give anger its due respect. The anger I held within ate at me from the inside out.

Then about a month into the divorce, my ex and I had a phone call. He just wanted to know how I was feeling. He told me to say anything, and he would just listen. And in that moment, a flood gate opened, and I let everything out. The anger poured out of me in an avalanche. I said everything. Everything I had held in for years, months, and especially over the previous few weeks.

It was like a pressure valve opened and all the weight I had sitting on my heart and my chest seemed to just fade away. Once I let my true anger out, I felt like I could breathe again for the first time in a long time.

Yes, my anger hurt him, but it was killing me. The anger had to get out or else it would have stayed in me. The anger would have followed me into future relationships where I eventually would have taken it out on people who didn't deserve it.

Be honest with yourself about the emotions you are actually experiencing, so you can truly feel them. Don't stuff them away because you're afraid of them or uncomfortable feeling them. They need to get out. They need to be felt.

Your emotions are there to help you navigate your life, and while you shouldn't follow them blindly into any situation, you should respect that each of them has their own timely and valuable purpose in your life.

If the idea of fully expressing your emotions is something you struggle with, I recommend seeing a therapist. Feeling our emotions can sometimes be too overwhelming to handle on our own, so sharing those emotions with others is a great way to learn how to unleash and manage them.

2. Embrace Loneliness

Sometimes to gain clarity about a situation, you need to step away from it and look inward. I don't mean that you should distract yourself with other people. Visiting friends, watching TV, reading a book, listening to music, or anything that involves the words of other people, while great ways to spend your time, are not pathways to the kinds of inward reflection we need to gain clarity.

This inward reflection requires you to talk with yourself. It means long drives alone with the speakers off. It means journaling. It means prayer. It means looking at the mirror when no one else is home. Looking inward means staying up in the dark talking out loud with your conscience.

Take the time to be alone, really alone, even if only for short chunks of the day.

Loneliness is a hard feeling for a lot of people, myself included. I don't do well with loneliness. It makes me very uncomfortable because I get no sense of fullness or validation from it. But I believe the discomfort of loneliness comes from the fact that it forces you to face yourself. When I am alone, I have nowhere to run and nothing to distract me from my uncomfortable thoughts and feelings.

Yet in facing myself, I am able to find clarity and ask myself the tough questions I'd otherwise leave unasked and unanswered.

For this act of self-love, set some time aside to just reflect. If this practice feels like too much, you can start with thirty minutes a week. Sit with yourself and ask yourself questions. Get to know yourself.

Here are some great questions to ask yourself:

- What are some of the core values or pillars I want to direct the decisions in my life? (Mine include faith, creativity, joy, love, independence, strength, and presence. I write these values down in my journal every morning).
- What brings me joy?
- What brings me pain?
- Who are some of the people in my life that I am truly happy being around?
- What do I like about myself?
- What's something I've never done but always wanted to do?
- When have I felt truly at peace? What factors helped create that peace? Which of those factors can I bring into my daily life?
- When was the last time I did something nice for myself?

3. Learn to Meditate

Great freedom and healing come with understanding that people are not bound to you. People will leave your life; people will die. You will leave other people's lives, and you will die. And that's okay. That's how life is supposed to be (or at the very least, it is what it is).

Becoming comfortable, or at least coming to grips with this fact of life, will allow you to appreciate the people in your life even more because you will no longer take people or your relationships for granted.

Learn to appreciate the moments you do have with the ones you love and be fully present in those moments. Stop counting on "forevers," because they simply do not exist. Be present in the moment, because all moments, good or bad, are only temporary. Time will pass and things will change.

Being present, in its simplest form, is meditation. But meditation does not just look like you humming to yourself with your legs crossed and palms open. Meditation means getting out of your thinking brain and into your senses.

Meditation requires actively listening to the sounds around you. Feeling the air come in and out of your lungs. Feeling the skin of the person holding your hand. Feeling the vibrations in their chest as they laugh and hearing the melody of the laughter as it quickly floats through the air. Smelling the oils in their hair or even the coffee on their breath. Feeling their chest expand and compress as they breathe next to you. Listening to the tick-tock of the clock and not thinking about the time passing, but instead just hearing the sound. Feeling the weight of your body as gravity pulls you into where you are sitting or lying down. Seeing the way the light silhouettes the face of a loved one in just the right way. Eating slowly so you can taste every ingredient that went into the meal they cooked.

Being present means being acutely aware of your existence in the space and moment you are in. It means getting out of your brain and into the world around you through the sensory powers of your body. If you don't appreciate the present moment, the world will change around you and you will have missed the intimate experience of it all because you were stuck inside your head thinking stupid thoughts instead.

Remember, meditation is a practice and not something anyone picks up very easily. It takes repeated practice to get more proficient. The first time I tried to meditate, my attention span lasted about ten seconds before I was back into thinking thoughts. Now, after years of practice, I can meditate completely for at least a few minutes or so. Be patient with yourself, but also don't skip this particularly powerful life skill.

4. Communicate Your Needs

Communicating your needs may require you to first figure out what your needs even are. This discovery will entail some seriously deep conversations with yourself. The easiest way to start is by determining your love language. Love languages are the way in which a person gives and receives love, which author Gary Chapman outlines in his amazing book, *The Five Love Languages.* I highly recommend this book because if the people in your life, especially your partner, do not know and actively engage your love language, it will be nearly impossible for you to feel loved by them.

Determining your love language is a good starting point but is not the only way to determine what your needs are. One other way is to keep a journal. In this journal you can keep track of your emotions and what triggers those emotions within you. By journaling, you will eventually recognize patterns within yourself of what heals you and what hurts you.

Once you have an idea of what some of your needs may be, it is crucial to verbally communicate those needs. Calling others out when those needs are not fulfilled or are ignored altogether is especially difficult for the people pleaser. This idea may seem so cliché, but communication is the only way someone else can understand what to do to be a better person for you. You have to articulate what you need from the people around you and hold them accountable for showing up for you per those needs. More on this subject in the next chapter.

5. Go Back to Chapter 1

A few weeks into the official end of my marriage I went on a hunt for eligible men. I wanted all the physical and emotional connection I could get from anyone who met my (not so high) standards. The plan was not to fall in love but was more about running. I simply needed a distraction.

Then over the next five or six months I slowed down and raised my standards even higher. I cried all the tears I had to cry and thought I was "moving on."

I got a new wardrobe, adorably dorky glasses, new eyebrows, better make up, and a new haircut. I was also just generally feeling better about myself and my life.

But I was still hunting. I was still running. Even though I thought I had "moved on," a part of me was still trying to prove to my ex, myself, and the world that I was worth more than the humiliating and traumatic way my marriage ended.

When all was said and done, I was still seeking validation from others.

It took some time (and to be completely straight forward, that stopwatch is still counting) for me to come full circle. For me to remember the ultimate message of this book and my life. My worth is unconditional.

If other people fail to show up for me, that is not a mark against my worth. If my relationship status isn't the pretty one we put in picture frames above the fireplace, that doesn't reduce my value. My worth remains as whole and as sturdy as it did the day I was born, with brand new eyes and all that innocence and potential.

My worth is in me, radiating at all times. It does not fade, and it does not die. And it sure as hell is not diminished simply because I'm single.

Part of the reason I was so gung-ho about dating so quickly after my divorce was (1) because I wanted a distraction from the pain, and (2) because I felt like I needed to prove to myself that people still wanted me, and that my worth could still be acknowledged by those around me.

But the question I had to ask myself was why I felt so stubbornly that for my worth to have meaning, it had to be acknowledged, appreciated, and wanted by a man. Why was it that my worth was not enough all on its own?

If a man isn't looking at me, does it mean I disappear? If I'm not in love with someone, has my life lost all purpose? If no man claims me as theirs, do I cease to exist? The answer to all three is a loud ass, "NO".

Yes, romantic love and connection are beautiful and powerful things that I want to cultivate in my life again. But I needed to make sure I was doing so for the right reasons.

I needed to make sure that the next go around, I didn't fall in love simply because I felt seen by someone, but also because all of my other, and just as important, needs were being met.

If you find yourself trapped in an inability to move on from an ex or find yourself constantly searching for the next guy to fill the role. Ask yourself why. Question your motives. Be real with yourself.

Learning to believe in our worth without external validation from others, and especially from significant others, is hard. But not as hard as living a life devoted to seeking wholeness through other people.

You can find wholeness, purpose, and love within yourself, and all by yourself. You just have to dig a little deeper.

CHAPTER 5

I Am Alone

I avoid acknowledging and facing my negative emotions. I lean on passive aggression and am terrified of direct confrontation. This fear manifests into hiding from people, lying about how I feel, and an overwhelming sense of loneliness.

In Chapter 1, I mentioned that anxiety is the product of your flight or fight instinct responding to imagined threats. In this chapter, however, we're going examine the fight or flight instinct responding to actual threats.

Without even a hint of hesitation, my response to real-life danger is always flight. If there is a threat to my safety or even my peace of mind, I run. And what counts as a "threat" for me is anything involving disapproval, negative emotions, or any kind of unpleasant behaviors.

These threats include everything from a driver flicking me off on the road, a co-worker telling me they are not impressed with my work, a friend being rude or inconsiderate to me, a stranger giving me a dirty look, a family member telling me I hurt their feelings, a loved one disrespecting me, an acquaintance making me uncomfortable, or a romantic partner ignoring my needs and boundaries.

Often, when uncomfortable situations like this happen, my immediate response is to get as far away from the person or situation as possible and hide. Common hiding places for me include but are not limited to: my car, closets, under my covers with a pillow clutched over my face, and bathrooms.

As an adult with a stable job, I've been able to get even more creative with my hiding spots. I've got the money and freedom to travel to wild and exotic places, drink alcohol, sleep for obnoxiously long periods of time, binge-watch TV for 12 hours, go on dates with skanky men, and do whatever it takes to distract myself from my feelings and disconnect from my reality.

This immediate flight response is how I reacted to other people's negative emotions or actions towards me, as well as from my own feelings of anger, frustration, or disapproval towards others. Not only was I unable to face the emotions of other people, but I also was unable to face my own emotions.

Typically, if I feel sad, angry, or frustrated with a person or issue, I choose to ignore the problem and "let it go." I put "let it go" in quotes, because by ignoring the problem I am doing everything *but* letting it go. What occurs instead is the exact opposite. The problem grows exponentially, and I become resentful towards others and towards myself because of it.

The longer this avoidance lasts, the larger the resentment, negative feelings, and behaviors become. The people in my life recognize that poor or disrespectful behavior are acceptable ways to interact with me, because I don't do anything about it. And I become angry with myself and with them over the fact that things aren't changing.

Yet when disappointments about my behavior are shared with me, I will feel mortified with the idea that I have displeased someone. Instead of facing the discomfort I caused others, I run and hide. I sweep the feelings away, and when the issue comes up in conversation with others or within myself, I quickly change the subject.

I just don't want to deal with any of this negativity. Can't we all just live in a world made of sugar and candy where all we feel is joy, peace, and pleasure? Why, oh why do there have to be all these other gosh-dang emotions?

This avoidance of my feelings, while momentarily effective, is frightfully destructive to my wellbeing and the relationships I create, whether professional, platonic, or romantic. This avoidance cultivates into a toxic monster called passive aggression.

For those who are unfamiliar with the term, passive aggression is a backhanded way of communicating. It typically looks like slamming doors, being sarcastic, audibly sighing, giving dirty looks, ignoring or blocking phone calls, throwing shade, talking about someone when they are not present, showing up late, giving the silent treatment, throwing things, making hurtful jokes or embarrassing comments to someone in front of other people, forgetting important dates, half-assing your duties, etc.

Passive aggression, at its core, is a cowardly way of showing your anger and frustration without having to confront that emotion or communicate about it.

In my personal life, the most destructive of all my passive aggressive behaviors was when someone asked what's wrong and I said, "Nothing. I'm fine." I was usually anything but fine and somehow expected the other person to intuit my real, hidden feelings, without me having to express them. My thinking was that they should just know that I'm not okay, I shouldn't have to explain it.

When someone says they are fine when they are not, not only are they rejecting the act of affection from the person checking in on them, but they are also rejecting their own truth which doesn't help anyone.

I cannot count the number of times I've said, "I'm fine," when I wasn't.

Back in the days when passive aggression was pretty much the only way I knew how to deal with difficult emotions, my husband at the time, whom I loved and trusted more than anyone, basically had to shake the truth out of me. He had to repeatedly ask me, "What's wrong? What's wrong? What's wrong? What's wrong?"

Being honest and upfront with others does not come naturally to me. It usually takes an extreme amount of conscious effort for me to confront a problem.

Passive aggression is an interesting beast, because I can be fully aware of its presence and its toxicity yet still fall into its addictive patterns. There have been times when I had an issue with someone and developed an entire plan and speech, ready to discuss the issue with them. I repeated the phrase, "Be an adult," in my head and out loud as I approached them. But when they looked at me and said, "So, are we going to talk about this or what?" I'd back down and say, "Talk about what? Nothing's wrong." And then walk away.

It is so frustrating that even when I want to, plan to, and fully intend to confront someone, I can still chicken out. In these instances, I allow my fear to control me instead of me controlling my fear.

This example is why I use the metaphor of addiction to discuss pleasing people, because it is an actual addiction for me and millions of others. When someone with a drinking problem goes into a bar and orders a drink, they know they don't need it, they know they shouldn't drink it, they know it brings harm to them and the people they love. But they get the drink anyway because in some fucked-up way, it seems like the safest action to take. I, like the alcoholic, very easily fall helplessly into my own self-defeating, toxic patterns.

Changing our patterns takes serious self-awareness and self-discipline, especially when our subconscious mind thinks those patterns protect us. I grew up thinking that I kept myself loved and safe by giving people what I believed made them happy and held back anything they might not like.

Standing up for myself, calling out bad behavior, or even just being honest about my own negative feelings were all actions I considered to be off-limits. Those emotions might make those around me uncomfortable or upset with me. And I simply couldn't bear to have anyone be upset, or worse, not like me.

I recently heard, "Honesty without kindness is brutality, and kindness without honesty is manipulation." In the past, I tended to see my inability to be honest with others as a good quality, because it makes me exceptionally "nice." However, after hearing this quote, I recognized that my "nice" was less about being kind and more about me trying to control other people's perceptions of me.

Further, when I allow all my honesty to bottle up, eventually it reaches a boiling point where I explode with "honesty" on people without any kindness in mind. When this outburst happens, I become be the epic bitch I so desperately tried to hide.

This kind of behavior endangers a person's wellbeing in several ways. First of all, if you are not willing to allow other people to see the real you or to be there for you, then no one will be able to. You need people in your life who you can be honest with.

When we aren't honest with others about our real selves, our struggles, and our needs that are not being met, this behavior can manifest into harmful bodily responses, like anxiety, loneliness, and immobility. We can easily get lost in the depths of our emotions and start to drown in them. During times like this, it is important to have someone there you can call for help to pull you out. If there is no one to pull you out, you may take drastic and irresponsible measures to claim control, like self-harm or careless adrenaline-seeking.

Being honest with the people in our lives is so crucial, not only to our relationships but also to our general wellbeing. Being honest about our flaws, failures, doubts we have, boundaries that need to be set, or the overwhelm we feel from constantly saying yes to people is very difficult for the people pleaser. We would rather pretend nothing is wrong. Shining lights on flaws makes us uncomfortable, and we're not really up for all that.

We don't want to upset other people by saying no or telling them how stressed out and overwhelmed we feel. People pleasers would rather suffer silently and continue to give away pieces of ourselves as though nothing is wrong. And this makes us, or at least me, feel incredibly alone.

I can have loads of people around me all of the time but still I feel like I have to carry this shit all by myself. I can even start to get angry and resentful at the people in my life for not understanding me, and then blame them for my feelings of loneliness.

But eventually, I realized that how I felt had absolutely nothing to do with the people in my life. They are not mind readers. They are not psychic. They are over here doing their very best to be there for me, yet I'm unable to see their support because I am caught up in my delusions of loneliness.

My loneliness really came down to an issue of trust. I didn't trust anyone in my life. I had a delusional mindset that if I made other people uncomfortable by sharing my discomforting thoughts with them, they would inevitably abandon me. And I would be left feeling even lonelier than I already felt.

As discussed, I tried to fill the void of loneliness by reaching for the wrong things. I was desperate for connection, attention, and love because I did not know how to cultivate those attributes within myself or within the already established relationships in my life.

My understanding of how to cultivate connection was to keep other people as happy with me as possible. This people pleasing required complete self-sacrifice in the name of other people's momentary feelings. I became terrified of other people's anger, disappointment, pain, and disconnection.

Over the last year in particular, I've strived to be more direct with the people in my life. I've worked at setting boundaries, clarifying my needs, and sharing my real thoughts and feelings. While this may seem simple to some people, it has been one of the hardest character transformations I have ever practiced.

During the days, weeks, and sometimes months leading up to a difficult conversation, I become consumed by a constant state of worry and anxiety. I have nightmares, panic attacks, and just straight-up bad vibes prior to and following a confrontation.

If all of this emotion seems a little dramatic to you, then good. Because it *is* super dramatic. It is completely childish for me to be so scared to ask for a little respect or help from the people in my life. But I am *that* scared. I am terrified of removing myself from a place of supposed safety in being the "nice" girl.

But "nice" simply wasn't working for me anymore. And beneath the microscope it turns out being "nice" was actually pretty mean to myself and those around me.

My inability to be honest with others also showed up in what is considered to be the most common of all the people pleasing patterns: an inability to say no. For me, this looked like saying yes to any request that was asked of me, even if I didn't have the means or desire to perform the favor. It meant giving my body, time, and resources to people who did not respect or value them.

When people asked me for something, whether it be a simple favor or my very soul, I gave it willingly. I desperately hoped this eagerness to give myself away would somehow take away the loneliness I constantly danced with. Yet when it didn't take away the loneliness, I hated myself all the more and clung to these patterns even more strongly.

The patterns got worse over time. I gave away money, time, and resources that I didn't have to spare. I allowed friendships and relationships to become emotionally painful and participated in activities I was not comfortable with. At my job, I took on roles I was never okay having.

In her book, *The Disease to Please,* Dr. Harriet Braiker said, "Before you can even think of a plausible reason to say no, the sheer force of habit from years of conditioning as a people pleaser makes your "yes" response pop out automatically. The weight of guilt, your constant emotional companion, holds you back from denying the favor. You conclude, as you always do, that it is just easier to say yes, than to find your way through the negative emotions that saying "no" seems to create. What you fail to realize however, is that by doing the favor, for which you have neither time nor desire, you will generate feelings that are even more difficult and threatening."

The more I work on my confrontation skills the more I realize how positive these momentarily negative conversations can be. By shutting down and holding back my truths, I subconsciously reinforce hateful self-beliefs that say my self-respect and wellbeing aren't worth the effort. These thoughts reinforce a belief that I am somehow unworthy. But by ending this pattern and sharing my truths (kindly) to those around me, I flip the script to one of personal worth, dignity, and power.

I'm learning to stand firm in my awareness of my worth. It is in this understanding of my (unconditional) worth that I know it is okay for me to tell others when they disappoint me, and it is also okay for others to tell me when I disappoint them. I do not need to run and hide, because I am safe in the darkness of all the negative emotions. I am safe because these interactions do not diminish my authentic light. I can stand in the darkness because I have light within me. These interactions do not determine my worth, but they do determine how I, and others, recognize and respond to my worth.

I am learning to replace fear with love. Nowadays when someone important to me asks how I'm doing, I really tell them how I'm doing instead of hiding behind, "I'm fine." Because those who hold honest love for me have earned the right to be there for me when they are able to and when I need them.

Instead of walking away, I stand firm. Instead of shutting down, I open up. Instead of crying ... well, let's not get too carried away, I still cry. After all, this shit is really hard for me.

Your understanding of your worth is what this really comes down to. Do you believe you and your happiness are worth the discomfort? Are you worth it? And if the answer isn't yes, then you have got some work to do.

I believe we should pick our battles and not start a fight over every last issue, but the big issues, the problems we mention to our friends repeatedly, the problems that give us anxiety as soon as we wake up and that keep us up all night, those issues need to be addressed. You are worth it.

Acts of Self-love to Practice

1. Verbalize Your Needs and Feelings

Although it sucks to admit, no matter how well a person knows us, they will never be able to read our minds. So, if you are trying to create a stable relationship with a person, yourself included, you have to be able to communicate with them about your honest feelings.

This practice is particularly hard for a people pleaser to master. Often, we would rather wallow in, and thus exacerbate, our own anger and frustration, rather than share those emotions with someone. This internal struggle is extremely counterproductive. When you don't communicate your emotions to anyone because you want to avoid the difficult feelings that come with conflict, you allow the original, difficult feelings within you to grow on a massive scale.

By avoiding outward conflict, you create internal conflict. This pattern of avoidance, which only aggravates the situation, becomes a vicious cycle and is extremely hard to break free from.

The way out of the cycle is to speak up.

Think about a situation or person in your life that causes you stress and journal about it. Figure out what you need from them that you are not getting, or what boundary you need to be set to keep the relationship healthy. Once you've shuffled through your thoughts and decided what the problem really is and what a possible solution could be, then comes the hard part.

Open your mouth and say the words. Do NOT hold on to the thoughts and hope the other person figures it out. They won't. If they haven't figured it out on their own yet, then they aren't about to any time soon.

You have to speak up for yourself.

This same practice can be done on an intrapersonal level. If you are hurting yourself and need to set boundaries with yourself or have needs from yourself that are not being met, talk to yourself about it.

It may seem totally kooky and dumb, but straight-up sit yourself down and talk to yourself. Set yourself straight. Be honest with yourself about what actions you do that hurt you, and what actions you are not doing that you know you need.

2. Give Other People Some Credit

Boo thang, trust me. I know what it is like to fear honesty as being dangerous and up to no good. I know how uncomfortable honesty is. I have been there in the space of being so stinking terrified of scaring, upsetting, or hurting the people around me that I chose to keep the truth inside. I chose to believe that they couldn't handle it, that I couldn't handle it. I believed that unleashing these truths I hoarded in my mind would somehow cause me to lose people.

Losing people sucks. Sitting in the fear of losing people sucks too. So instead, you just decide being honest is too risky. The truth could ruin your day and it's hard enough just getting through the day without adding truth bombs to the mix.

But if you have someone in your life, be it a friend, a family member, a partner, or whoever that you consider a solid and needed presence in your life, you have to give them the benefit of the doubt. You have to believe that honesty will not make them disappear. You have to give them some dang credit, that maybe your relationship is deeper than surface-level bull shit. Maybe they will be there for you, even if you say something that makes them uncomfortable. Even if you say some shit that they didn't want to hear.

And the truth is, if this person is unable to hear your truth and still be there for you, then they were never really there for you to begin with. It was a surface-level relationship. And if that's the case, go back to the previous chapter to see how to let that bitch go.

Don't get me wrong. Surface-level relationships can be fun and easy. And there's no real harm in having a couple of those in your life. But if surface-level relationships are all you have, or if they are the relationships that take up most of your time, then loneliness is a guarantee. If you are searching for something more, then you need to create deeper relationships. And that requires authenticity, honesty, and depth.

3. Be Selfish

The past year has come with massive changes. I have spoken to various people about treating me with more respect, I've set clear boundaries with others, and I ended some relationships altogether. Following each of these experiences, I felt flooded with guilt and shame as though I'd done something horrifically wrong, even though I knew I had done what was best for me.

The feeling of cutting someone off or refusing to give them what they want goes against everything I once believed made me a "good" person. So, if I don't fit in with my definition of a "good" person, then it means that I must be a "bad" person. Right?

Harriet Braiker said, "While people pleasers may think they excel at making other people happy, their real talent lies in making themselves feel miserable and inadequate.... As a people pleaser, you push yourself around with commanding orders, burden yourself with a strict code of personal rules, and measure yourself against unrealistic judgmental standards. And you do all this in order to be a nice person. But why can't you be nice to yourself?"

The most barf-inducing word in the people pleaser's vocabulary is "selfish." Selfish is the last thing on Earth we would ever want to feel like or be characterized as, especially by others. The very thought makes me sick to my stomach.

But here's the T: if you don't take care of you, then who is going to? You have got to care about your needs. You matter. Your happiness matters. My God, you are a freaking source of light, love, and energy, and it's time you show yourself the respect you deserve! This is not about how other people show up for you, or how you show up for other people. This is about how you show up for yourself.

Your emotions will not settle on their own. Your boundaries will not set themselves. Your anger will not fly away. Your needs will not meet themselves. You have to step up and take care of yourself.

I'm not saying go around only caring about yourself, throwing all your emotional baggage onto the people around you, and flicking off the rest of the world with bitterness and constant angst. I'm saying, listen to your emotions when they come up. Do not push them away. Listen to your inner dialogue. Have the conversations you are scared of. Believe that you are worth it.

Think of yourself as a friend. Or, better yet, think of yourself as a child. You are a kid who needs love, attention, and for someone to treat them as though they and their needs matter.

You are not "asking for too much." Just by being human, you deserve to have needs and to have those needs met. Understanding this fact doesn't make you selfish, it means you have self-awareness and self-respect.

4. Ask for Help

Many people I know see asking for help as a weakness. But admitting that we need support is far from inadequacy. True weakness is being too scared to admit failure, setbacks, or pain, so that you spend your life suffering all alone.

Asking for help, in both small and big ways, is in fact one of the bravest things a person can do. Whether you're asking for help with household chores like laundry or shoveling the snow off your driveway, or asking for support and solidarity in the journey to sobriety, both acts bring reality to your internal understanding that your needs matter and that you are not superhuman.

Sometimes, taking responsibility for your life looks like asking for help. Gaining control involves communicating honestly with the people you do have or finding someone with whom you can communicate honestly.

One of the concerns that held me back from asking for help in the past is that I wasn't entirely sure what kind of help I needed. I didn't know what my needs were. I didn't know what to ask for.

I've discovered that communicating with others is not always about knowing what you need or knowing what to say but is more about letting others know that you are in need at all. True communication is about the very act of simply reaching out. Then conversations will build, and you can begin to figure out what your needs are as you open discussion with others.

The key point is that it's incredibly difficult to figure out life all on your own. And self-inflicted loneliness is an unnecessary and shitty thing to put yourself through.

Many of us who grew up in difficult childhoods tend to cling to this idea that we got ourselves through all of our early onset hardships, so we can get ourselves through everything else on our own too. And while there is so much power in recognizing your power to overcome the difficulties in your life, there is also power in having company along the way.

Human beings are social animals. We need other people. Your feeling of overwhelm because you can't do everything on your own is not unique to you. That is a universal experience. We need each other. So, reach out, be open, and be willing to accept the love others want to give you.

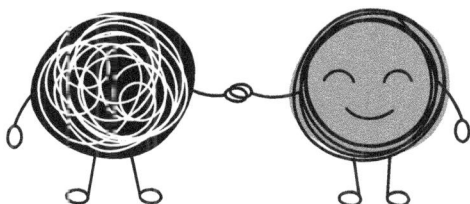

CHAPTER 6

I Am Sorry

Self-compassion and self-forgiveness do not come easy to me. I am extremely critical of myself and my mistakes. I hold grudges against myself and am my own worst bully.

People pleasers say "I'm sorry" too much. It's to the point that when I bump into a chair, I apologize to the chair. Replacing the words "I'm sorry" with more confident ways of acknowledging our mistakes or thanking others for their patience and help is important. But I'm not going to waste this chapter talking about our word choice. I'm going to go a little deeper. I'm going to go to the places of internal self-contempt that we do not acknowledge. I'm going to talk about the kinds of mistakes that fundamentally change how we see ourselves.

In civil society, most people want to be a "good" person. Of course, what defines a "good" person is fluid, subjective, learned, and context based. Regardless, people pleasers tend to determine for themselves at a young age what defines a "good person" and create personal behavioral guidelines based on these definitions.

When we go through our lives and act in ways that are outside of the strict lines we set for being "good," we rely on self-punishment to put us back in place.

Punishment for wrongdoing is the way of life in America. Punishment is how we respond to fuck ups, big or small. Ideally, it is the fear of punishment that then keeps us from willingly fucking up or doing fucked-up things. Self-punishment in particular is a tool we develop over our lifetimes because we believe it helps sculpt us into "better" people.

Often, self-punishment can look like prolonged feelings of guilt and shame, obsessing over mistakes in your head, physically hurting yourself, calling yourself "a piece of shit," "stupid," "no good," or "a screw up," and withholding yourself from both pleasures and necessities, such as food, rest, or in the worst cases, love or connection with others.

While it may seem counterintuitive, self-punishment is actually a form of defense. It is meant to protect us from the consequences of future mistakes and to repent (whether you are religious or not) from the consequences of past mistakes.

Self-punishment is the mind's way of recognizing the harm you've caused, **whether real or perceived**, and encouraging you to never cause that same harm again. In theory, self-punishment is effective, valuable, and honorable. We should feel bad when we do bad. That's what keeps us good. Or at least that's how life is supposed to work.

In an ideal world, when we mess up or make a poor decision, a consequence arises. Then we feel bad, we punish ourselves, we learn a lesson, we feel better, we don't make that same mistake again, and the self-punishment stops. But we don't live in an ideal world. We live in the real world, where shit is so much more complicated.

To get through this chapter, I need to define a few terms.

The first terms are guilt and shame. Guilt and shame are often mistaken for each other because they tend to show up at the same time, but they are vastly different. Guilt is a negative emotion you feel when you've done something against your own moral code of what qualifies as "good" behavior. Shame, however, is an emotionally negative evaluation of yourself as a whole person. In other words, guilt says, "I *did* something bad," and shame says, "I *am* bad."

Guilt is of the moment, and shame is of the ego. But what exactly is the ego? Basically, the ego is the part of your personality that makes decisions based on attempts to satisfy your needs and wants within the boundaries of your own moral context. In even simpler terms, the ego is your self-awareness. The ego is your perception of who you are.

Mastering the ego is really what this book is all about. Because it is the ego that tells us we are unworthy. It is the ego that tells us to look for worth in other people. It is the ego that breaks us down and holds us back from truly loving ourselves. However, the good news is that the ego is flexible and can be transformed. It is through the transformation and releasing of our egos that we can learn to breathe life into the concept of unconditional worth.

When your ego goes unchecked and untamed, it can force you to participate in toxic and unhelpful forms of self-punishment. For a while, my ego told me I was annoying and that to be "good," I needed to be quiet. As I stated in Chapter 2, this belief was extremely unhealthy for me and took a whole lifetime to recover from.

For others, their egos may tell them that to be "good" they need to be skinny and that they should starve themselves to be so. The ego can convince someone that they are not capable of being loved wholly and will force them to sabotage good relationships or seek out unhealthy partners.

The ego can say you're a terrible person for hurting someone you loved, or it can convince you that you aren't worthy of forgiveness. Your ego will tell you that you fucked up, and therefore you are fucked up and should be punished. The ego is where self-punishment and the inability to forgive or trust ourselves comes from. So, it is through awareness of how our egos function that we can and must learn how to let go of these patterns.

Some of you may be thinking, "But I like punishing myself. It helps me, it makes me a better person, and it makes me feel better about the mistakes I've made." But when we punish ourselves for mistakes, we only strengthen the toxic power of our egos which is simply a fictitious perception of ourselves. This penance does not strengthen our actual selves. Through self-punishment we focus on the needs of the ego and not the needs of our inner children and authentic selves.

I've participated in a lot of self-punishment throughout my life. I've also had a lot of "good reasons" to punish myself.

I've been selfish, lazy, manipulative, dismissive, self-absorbed, narcissistic, one-sided, ignorant, arrogant, judgmental, and petty. I've neglected and shamed people whom I loved. I've intentionally used people. I've let people down who were counting on me. I've turned a blind eye to injustice, prejudice, societal flaws, and crimes against humanity. I've stolen things (many, many things), sped way too fast down quiet neighborhood streets, driven when I should not have been behind the wheel, ran stop signs and red lights, defaced public property, and committed lots of other non-law-abiding acts.

I've also embarrassed myself, failed at tasks, quit on my commitments, lied too many times to count, broken promises, looked a mess, been abusive to myself, let people take advantage of me, fallen down, and settled.

I've made a lot of choices which I am not proud of. And I've chastised myself physically, verbally, and mentally for those regretful choices. But eventually, I realized that all that self-punishment did was weaken me. Every time I yelled at myself or called myself stupid, I created self-resentment in place of self-love.

When I punished myself, I upheld the misguided perception that I should be ashamed of who I am. By affirming these perceptions of shame, I set myself up for future failure, because I strengthened an ego that believed I was already a shameful person. This ego made decisions for me based on this skewed perception of myself

In an effort to protect you, the ego will create an image of you that is harsh and inaccurate. It will force you to lower your standards for what you believe you deserve or what you think you are capable of and will set you up to repeat past mistakes.

Let's start with a small example. When I get called out for a mistake in a work meeting, the first feeling I have is embarrassment and guilt, "Whoops! Guess I messed up." But then it is typical for these feelings to evolve into full-blown shame as I fixate on how stupid everyone in the meeting must think I am because I am a person who messes up. I then start to think I don't belong with these people who are so much better at their jobs than me. And then every consecutive time I mess up after that, I add it to the pile of proof that I am just stupid. This idea turns into self-doubt which then messes with my psyche and causes me to make more mistakes in the future.

It's easy to see how in small situations like these, through awareness and practice, a person could and should quickly learn from the mistake, let it go, and not allow it to alter their ego. They should simply recognize a negative spiral and be conscious of it so they can prevent it from getting too dark.

But what about the bigger mistakes? What about the choices that landed you in prison, tore apart your marriage, traumatized your child, got you fired, destroyed your career, ended a friendship, disappointed your parents, led you to bankruptcy, killed someone, or in some other way totally ruined your life? What about mistakes like that? The really big ones. You should be ashamed of doing really bad things, right? In these situations, don't you deserve to be punished?

Where is the line drawn? At what point, amid the punishment of self, is it morally, psychologically, and socially righteous to let the penance go and walk in the waters of forgiveness?

You'd think that both religion and politics are mandatory components in answering this question, but this isn't that kind of book. This is a book about love, specifically self-love. And as a student of self-love, I have to say that the line for when it's okay to forgive yourself is drawn wherever and whenever you decide to draw it.

Guilt, in temporary, short-lived spurts, can teach you valuable lessons on becoming the kind of person you want to be. But shame and long-lived guilt that last for years are detrimental to your wellbeing. They feed into a completely twisted ego that does not believe in you and will consistently sabotage you. The ego won't even give you the chance to do better.

In 1988, Oprah Winfrey invited Dave Mazzella, the Vice President of the Aryan Youth Movement (a white supremacy group) and some of his group members on her show in the hopes of having a productive dialogue and an edgy, controversial episode. Throughout the episode, the guests spewed hate and disgust towards her and all black people. Oprah regretted the choice to have them on her show and promised to never give that sort of hate a platform again. Until she invited them back on her show in 2011, 23 years later. In this later episode, these same people publicly apologized for how they acted and said they learned better and were different people now. Oprah uses this story to express my favorite quote of hers, "Once you know better, you do better."

"Doing better" requires letting go of the circumstances you cannot change. You cannot change the past. You cannot change what you did or didn't do. And you most certainly cannot punish yourself hard enough or long enough to change anything that happened in the past. You cannot be in control of your life if you allow past mistakes or regrets to have control over you.

Making mistakes teaches us so much about ourselves and the kinds of people we want to be or the kinds of lives we want to live. We should respect our mistakes for the lessons they taught us, decide how we will show up differently from this point on, and then let the shame and the guilt go.

I recognize that guilt, anger, and shame are appropriate human responses to terrible life events. But refusing to work through those responses and instead letting them cloud your mind and completely contort your perception of yourself is like drinking poison.

Now, I'm not suggesting that you will completely forget or fully disconnect from regrettable life events that you've experienced, but you can and must take control of your ego. Just because you made some bad choices, it doesn't mean you are a bad person.

I am so grateful for my mistakes. Yes, they sucked. Yes, if I could go back and not make terrible choices I would. But I can't. Even if time travel wasn't the stuff of science fiction, I can't go back and make different choices. Because if I did go back, I would make those same stupid choices over again. After all, the me at that time didn't know any better. But the me in this time does. And the only reason I know better now is because of the mistakes I made then that showed me the kind of person I didn't want to be.

To truly forgive yourself, you must take ownership of the mistakes you made and the choices you regret, then begin to hold yourself accountable for better behavior in the present moment.

Guilt and shame do not change you. What changes you are the choices you make. These choices can be made with or without guilt and shame. You don't need to hold on to these emotions once you have already learned from the lesson. The only time guilt and shame are remotely healthy is when you haven't yet learned from the lesson.

These emotions are healthy in getting you to the point of realization, but once you understand and decide to act differently, they are purposeless. At that point, self-punishment serves only your skewed self-defeating ego.

Recently, a loved one said something that knocked me on my ass. "Maybe you are a demon. But you are trying to be an angel. Don't you think God sees that?" Changing your behavior, making choices to be better, living in growth and self-awareness, taking responsibility for who you are and how you live your life, those efforts matter.

It matters that you are trying. It matters that you can look back on your past self and say, "I am not that person anymore."

In the grand scheme of things, no matter what beliefs you have about the soul, the universe, or life itself, who you choose to be right now, in this moment, matters.

Stop sabotaging yourself. Believe in your worth. Believe that your worth is unconditional and start making steps to breathe life into the kind of person you really want to be.

Acts of Self-Love to Practice

1. Affirm Yourself

Here we go again with the freaking affirmations. But hey, they really do work.

So, say it with me

"I accept that I am flawed. I accept ownership of my past. And I choose to let it go. My mistakes will not haunt me; they will guide me. I choose to move forward. I choose to move forward. I choose to move forward."

This affirmation signifies the release of your guilt and the action to make better choices. This affirmation thanks your guilt for showing you the light, and then releases it.

Self-punishment will not save you. Changing your choices will.

2. Talk with Your Inner Critic

My inner critic, that dumb cruel voice in my head that makes me cringe every time she speaks, tells me that I am stupid, annoying, selfish, a liar, a sinner, spoiled, self-adsorbed, and an all around boring terrible person. I am none of these, but I still think these words in my head on a regular basis. Sometimes when I have these thoughts, I have to talk out loud to myself and say, "That isn't true. I know who I am, and I love who I am."

Whatever your inner critic tells you, do not run from it. Bring those ideas out, write the thoughts down in a journal and talk them out. Ask yourself why you think this way, then challenge the thoughts. Argue with them. Stick up for yourself, even if your defense is against yourself.

Don't allow yourself to be bullied by anyone, especially you. This critic may never go away, but when it shows up, do not let it mess with your understanding of who you are or the unconditionality of your worth.

3. Honor Your Word

Once you say, "I forgive you," you better mean it.

In general, it is unfair and uncool to tell someone you forgave them when you really did not. That's the kind of "keeping the peace" decision that always comes back to bite you in the ass. Eventually, that hidden resentment will show itself, and you will have to answer for it. People have every right to believe you when you say you have forgiven them, so don't say it unless you plan to whole-heartedly commit to it.

The same goes with forgiving yourself. Once you decide to let your mistakes go, you better actively work and do whatever is necessary to let them go. There is no point in lying to yourself. If you are not ready to forgive yourself, it means you have not learned all that you needed to learn. So, sit in the discomfort, in the guilt, in the pain, and figure out what you need to learn. Then, let that stupid shit go.

4. Wish Yourself Well

There are many different definitions of forgiveness. But what most of them have in common is an increased ability to wish the offender well, regardless of if you believe they deserve wellness or not.

In his book, *Bird Uncaged*, prison abolitionist Marlon Peterson, after serving a ten-year prison sentence for a robbery that resulted in two murders, wrote, "How many times would I have to prove to people that I was no longer that nineteen year old boy?... Did I deserve the right to imagine freedom? The four people shot, the two who died, the neighborhood that was traumatized by the shooting --- they all suffer still... The prison that I have the hardest time identifying and abolishing is the one that has convinced me that I do not deserve to be happy; that happiness is a fleeting moment, but never a movement."

Even if you have fucked up or have done some fucked-up things, you are still worthy of love. You must remember that your worth is unconditional. Your worth and your value have not diminished due to bad choices. However, your worth will not manifest into a better life unless you choose to love yourself. Sure, if you're a masochist and think you're better off living a petty, bitter, childish life of misery and regret, then by all means, go for it.

But if you really want to become a better person, you achieve that desire through healthy, life-affirming, love-filled choices. You atone by putting good energy, good actions, and a good life into this world. You don't redeem yourself by punishing yourself, sitting in a dark room, drinking all night, crying yourself to sleep, and begging other people for forgiveness that may or may not ever come.

To atone for your past mistakes, you have to wish yourself well and become the kind of person who learns from their mistakes and decides to be a better person.

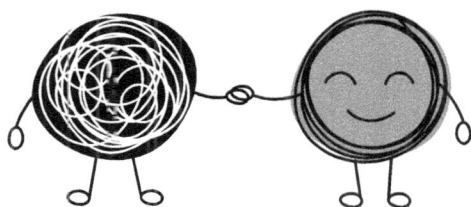

CHAPTER 7

I Don't Know Who I Am

My authentic self gets lost in the depths of my emotions and the emotions of those around me. I forget who I am and allow myself to fall victim to toxic inner thoughts and toxic communication from others.

A few months into my divorce, I felt sad. No, let me rephrase that. A few months into my divorce, I felt severely depressed. I stopped showing up for work. I stopped working on this book. I was behind on school projects. I stopped working out and waking up. I slept for most of the day. When I wasn't asleep, I was either crying or staring at the wall. I stopped praying, showering, journaling, cooking, cleaning, and taking care of myself in general. I sent just enough emails, answered just enough phone calls, and accomplished just enough to keep up the appearance that I was still alive.

People pleasers in general have an unmatched ability to seem "okay" when we are anything but okay. I, in particular, became very skilled at masking my emotions and putting on a positive attitude in all my interactions so as not to worry or upset other people. What's so ridiculous is that people pleasers are so good at masking our pain that we are capable of even hiding it from ourselves. We can believe we are "fine" when, in reality, we are barely holding on to life by a thread.

On January 10th, 2021, I wrote out a journal entry that said:

"Here I sit.

Barely able to breathe or keep my eyes open.

I am not okay.

I think of killing myself every day.

The wish to die plays on a loop in my head all day long.

My passions become less and less important to me.

I don't even care if I finish my book at this point.

I don't care if I get fired.

I don't care if I do a triathlon or not.

Or have kids

Or fall in love again...

I'm okay with dying tonight.

I'm sorry to everyone who believed in me.

I'm sorry to myself.

But I just don't want to do this anymore.

I'm tired.

I'm sorry.

I know you may never forgive me.

Because this is as selfish as it gets...

I'm not going to kill myself...

Right?"

The days surrounding this journal entry were filled with "curiosity-based" google searches on the best methods to take your own life. Since suicide prevention is such a big deal, finding this information took a lot more digging than you'd think.

Yet, I dug and compared the various methods. "If" I were to take my life, I'd want it to be painless and with the least amount of mess, in case a loved one had to identify my body. I didn't want to cause any extra trauma for others than what was necessary.

"Hypothetically," I thought out where I would go. It would have to be somewhere far enough away that none of my loved ones would find my body, but not so secluded that my body would never be found. Somewhere peaceful, like a beach.

I decided who would take care of my pets. I planned who would receive the life insurance and what little savings I had in my bank account.

Somewhere along line of hypotheticals and "what ifs," I started getting excited. I started getting more and more specific with the details. Eventually I realized it wasn't just a curious thought, it was a plan. But by that point I was so deep into the delusion of suicide as the solution to my problems that it was sort of out of my control.

I laid on the hardwood floor of my home office, staring at the white painted ceiling as I played the scene over and over again in my head of it all just fading to black. Death seemed so peaceful and so alluring.

I've always been a woman of action. When I get the idea to do something I usually either do it or let the idea go. I don't sit on dreams. So, I asked myself in my head, "Are we doing this or what?"

I thought about my mom and my family. I thought about my ex-husband. I thought about my friends. I thought about the hurt my suicide would inflict and the possible chain reactions it would cause. But at the time, I just didn't care. Love seemed so irrelevant when all I wanted was peace from the chaos in my head.

It all just seemed so pointless: working, growing, learning, surviving, and trying so hard just to be smushed like a bug anyways. Life didn't give a shit about me, why should I give a shit about it?

Then I started thinking about this book. I thought about the hopes I had for my message of self-love. I thought about the fact that no one would read my book if I killed myself before I could finish it. I thought about the woman who wrote again and again how you have to believe in your own worth. It is you who has to show up for yourself.

I thought about my hypocrisy.

The words slipped out in a sigh, "Who the fuck am I?"

And with that question, I pulled myself up off the floor and with tears streaming down my cheeks, I drove across town to my general care doctor's office. I requested an emergency meeting and luckily was able to get one. The nurse came into the room and asked me the reason for my visit, and I told her, "I'm having dangerous thoughts and I need help."

My doctor came in a few minutes later and sat with me for about 20 minutes. He helped me come up with a plan to cleanse my mind. He prescribed me some anti-depressants and told me about some books I should read.

But the most important thing he gave me was a simple statement. "You haven't been conditioned to handle emotional crises, but this is something you can learn. You are feeling hopeless and lost. But you are not hopeless. You are not lost. The fact that you came here today says it all. You know who you are. You are going to be okay."

Whether positive or negative, emotions have the power

to be all-consuming. We people pleasers in particular have an unbalanced relationship with our emotions. We are afraid of our negative emotions and try to avoid and escape them. We are obsessed with positive emotions and chase them, even when it leads to unhealthy choices. We have the capacity to be completely overwhelmed and consumed by our emotions so that we let them control and define us.

But emotions are just reactions to our experiences. They are not who we are. In the same way that we shouldn't allow other people's anger, disappointment, or judgment to diminish our sense of self-worth, we should also not allow our own emotions to change how we show up for ourselves or how we show up in the world.

I felt broken, so I decided I was broken and would be better off just giving up. But I was never broken, I was just hurting. But hurt can heal. And the me I knew before all this turmoil would show up again, wiser and stronger. Emotions are temporary, but who you are is separate from what exists within your mind and within your body. You are something so much deeper than your physical and emotional experience.

You are a light, a life force, an energy.

When my suicidal fantasies were disrupted by thoughts of my book, I questioned who I was. I asked myself, am I really the strong, love-filled, powerful woman I say I am in this book, or am I just a sad, broken fraud? At that moment, I made a choice. I chose to believe in my light, even though I couldn't see it at the time. I chose love.

I believe the strongest affirmational statement we can say to ourselves and to others is, "I know who I am." In this statement we deny the power of internal and external judgments and emotions to cloud the love we have for our authentic selves.

As people pleasers, we have a rough go at life. It usually takes some sort of trauma or magical moment for us to recognize our value and our worth. Until that season of awakening, we stew in this idea that we are replaceable, fragile, insignificant beings that constantly have to prove our value to others and this planet.

We are unable to claim a strong stance in our definition of ourselves and our worth. We just let the world shape us into what it chooses and pretend we have no control over who we are. But this notion is false.

We have so much control over who we are and how we show up in this life. We have so much power and so much light, but sometimes we are just simply blind to our worth. I refuse to be blind to my light any longer.

I still have harmful thoughts sometimes. They creep up when I'm feeling overwhelmed or lonely. I can't control the fact that these thoughts come to me. But I can control how I react to those thoughts. I no longer allow them to manipulate me into planning out my suicide. Instead, I let the thoughts come, I allow the pain to be felt for a short time, and then I journal. I get the thoughts out and don't get angry at myself for thinking them. Instead, I thank myself for choosing not to follow the thoughts down darker roads.

I haven't removed anger, fear, or sadness from my life. But I have added more love. More compassion, patience, and forgiveness. I know who I am, and I am not a person who will self-destruct because I choose not to be. I know who I am and therefore, I will no longer be controlled by ridiculous thoughts, no matter what they may be.

In the same sense that I don't allow myself to be pushed around by my own thoughts or feelings, I also don't allow myself to be pushed around by other people. Not anymore. When people attack, belittle, disrespect, judge, mock, or hurt me. I process what they've said and either allow it to add to my character or I let it go. However, I absolutely re-fucking-fuse to allow other people to skew my perception of myself and my life for the worse.

It goes against everything people pleasers are conditioned to believe about life and relationships to simply reject other people's targeted emotional violence. We believe our job is to take other's negative emotions and turn them into positive ones. We believe other people's thoughts and feelings are our responsibility.

But honestly, I'm so over it. I have worked too hard to create the solid footing I have on the ground just for someone else's emotions to come and knock me down. Not anymore. I am a woman who stands tall and firm in the knowledge of who she is.

I am not my thoughts. I am not my body. I am not my pain. I am not other people's thoughts, emotions, or pain. I am something completely other. I am love.

Acts of Self-Love to Practice

1. Be Graceful with Yourself

Running a marathon was more than just signing up for the race and showing up on race day. It took months of practice and training. I got all the way up to running a 19-mile distance in my training, just seven miles short of the whole marathon. And then I injured my foot from training too hard, and had to wait more than a month for it to heal, only to start training all over again at stage one.

My point? Just because you want to feel like a brand-new person today doesn't mean you will. Just because you've worked on yourself for years doesn't mean you won't have setbacks. It doesn't mean you won't have to keep training to stay in shape.

When I say your self-love should be unconditional, I mean it. Even when you're falling apart. Even when you don't recognize yourself anymore. Even when you're embracing all of the worst parts of yourself. Even when you are unhealthy and in pain. Even then, you need to love yourself, in all your cringy glory.

A person I follow on Instagram who goes by @dutchdeccc once said, "I've been seeing a lot of posts this month of people saying things like, 'it gets better' or 'it gets easier' and while I totally understand the potential impact those people are trying to have with those posts, I think it's also important to say that if things aren't getting better or they're getting worse, you still have value and you're still important. I think sometimes there's this thinking in mental health that things getting better looks like your mental health problems going away, and that might not be true. You might live alongside them for a while and that's okay. You don't have any less value because of that ... No matter where you are in the continuum of your mental health you are worth it, and you have value."

When you take any sort of difficult steps, especially soul-searching, personal-growth type work, it is easy to beat yourself up because you are not as far along as you wanted to be. Or maybe you fall back and have a bad day. You think, "I thought I was past this issue. I thought I was better than this." Or maybe you compare your growth to other people's growth.

Just chill. I call self-love a practice because, big surprise, it is, in fact, something you have to practice. It's not an item you buy that stays the same shape no matter how often you use it.

It is a living breathing part of you that needs to be respected and nourished.

And since it is not an inanimate object, setbacks can happen. Dips and curves in your growth journey are inevitable. So be kind and patient with yourself. Even if it feels like you're moving backwards, as long as your gaze is pointed in the right direction, that is the direction you will follow.

2. Admire Yourself

It's okay to be proud of how far you've come. It's okay to be inspired by how far you want to go. And since you are reading this book, you are probably a pretty cool person who is just trying to figure out yourself. So, in the process of finding yourself, take some moments to just say, "Dang. I am awesome!"

While finishing this book, I repeatedly felt overwhelmed and filled with anxiety. I asked my therapist how to enjoy the process instead of getting swept away in the stress and anxiety of it all. He said, "Take a moment, step back, and admire what you have done. Meditate on the feeling of what this work has meant to you. And how awesome you think it is. Hang it on your fridge like a work of art and just have a moment of admiration for yourself. Hold onto that feeling. It's okay to be anxious. But don't let that overpower the good you have felt."

With this advice in mind, pick something about yourself that you think is great. It could be your sense of style. Maybe it's your humor. Maybe it's a piece of art you made. Maybe it's the relationship you have with your cat. Maybe it's the fact that you finally kept that one house plant alive. Or maybe the part of yourself that you admire is a goal you haven't even achieved yet, but you're actively working for. Maybe you admire the fact that you read this whole book (kudos to you).

It doesn't matter what aspect of yourself and your life that you choose, but that part has to be something you genuinely think is cool. Take that piece of you and admire it.

Hold onto that feeling when circumstances get rough. Keep it in your back pocket and pull it out when you need a reminder that you are actually fucking awesome.

3. Get Your Facts Straight

Say it with me:

I am worthy because my worth is unconditional.

I will not be whoever you want me to be,
because I choose to be my authentic self.

I cannot save you because I need to save myself.

I do not need you, because I have me.

I am not alone, because I am surrounded by love.

I am sorry, and I forgive myself because
I've grown from my mistakes.

I know who I am because I choose love over fear.

I will leave you with this affirmation:

"Life will throw things at me, and I will get hurt sometimes. Sometimes I will trip and fall over my own feet. But even when times are dark, I am always able to find myself again because I am a light. I feel my light. I believe in my worth, unconditionally. I am so grateful to be exactly who I am. I will continue to appreciate myself for everything I am and everything I choose to be. I am filled with love. The time has come to access this love, let it flow through me and out into the world around me."

Let's grow together y'all.

Acknowledgments

Many people had a hand in helping me complete and release this first book of mine.

First, I have to give a big shout out to my therapist, the guy who led me to most of the realizations and insights I share in this book. I don't think I'm legally allowed to share his name with y'all, but the shout out is no less significant. You're an amazing person, great at your job, and I'm lucky to have you in my corner.

Next, thank you mom, for all that you do. You do more for me and our family than I could ever notate in any book. Thank you for not only letting me include your story in mine, but for also holding me accountable to complete this book. There were times when I considered it just too big of a project. You stepped in and reminded me that no project is too big for me. You reminded me, as you always have, that I am capable of anything. I thank you so much for being in my life and allowing me to live it on my own terms.

I also want to thank my Grandma Baker. You can't possibly understand just how inspirational you are to me. You have always been a shining example of what it means to take life on with spunk, dignity, and a can-do attitude, regardless of what happens. You taught me by example what it means to put yourself out there, reach for more, and act on your dreams. I thank you so much for being my friend, supporting me through every step I took in my life, and showing me what honest and authentic love really amounts to.

Thank you to my friends for checking in, cheering me on, and never letting me forget just how loved I am.

I also need to thank my ex-husband. Your enthusiasm, support, and confidence in me while I wrote this book meant the world to me. Being able to share my ideas with you and work out my thoughts with you filled me with immense love and appreciation. With that being said, I also need to thank you for the various lessons I share in this book that I learned both from and because of you. Some of these lessons were learned in love and joy while others were learned in heartbreak. But they all formed and shaped me as a person, nonetheless. I will love you always, even if that love looks and feels so much different than we planned.

Next up, thank you to my entire family. Thank you for putting aside your anxieties to support me in releasing this book. I realize through sharing my story, I share a piece of our entire family with everyone who reads it. Thank you for having my back and believing in me and my message.

Thank you to my editor Andrea McCurry for helping me make sense of my sometimes chaotic and rambling thoughts. Your patience and support have meant more than you know.

Thank you to my graphic designer Jennifer Stimson for creating an image and brand that fit so beautifully with the message and vibe I wanted to express.

Thank you to Brian Baker of Sound Arts Recording Studio for helping comfort and guide me through the daunting process of recording my own audio book. The audio would have been a mess had it not been for your patience, kindness, and leadership.

I want to also quickly give a shout out to author and coach DeAnne Joy. We don't know each other well, but your words stretched further for me than you could imagine. Thanks for encouraging me to expand my ideas of what is possible and reminding me that this whole book writing thing really isn't all that complicated.

And, I can't leave out Rachel Hollis. Rachel, while I have mixed feelings about some of your messages, I cannot deny that four years ago, *Girl, Wash Your Face* was the book that helped to light the long-lost writer match sitting in my soul waiting to be remembered and re-lit. Your bravery paved the way for mine.

Lastly, I want to thank you, the reader of this book. Thank you for hearing out the words of wisdom from some 26-year-old, 5'2" Texas girl, wanting so badly to find her own way by helping you find yours. I will forever and always believe that the best way to do anything is to do it with someone else.

I made up a little slogan when I started my Kind of Cathartic blog that said, *Let's Grow Together.* It has been the basis on which I live my entire life and will continue to be for as long as I can hold on to it. We accomplish so much more when we grow together than when we walk alone.

Thank you.

Note From the Author

If you enjoyed this book (or even if you didn't) please visit the site where you purchased it and write a brief review. Not only are reviews essential to book sales, but your feedback is important to me and will help other readers decide whether or not to read the book too.

And in the words of Erykah Badu, "now keep in mind that I'm an artist and I'm sensitive about my shit!"

About the Author

Often found in her Texas home typing away for her day job as a Marketing Coordinator and her night hustle as a writer, **Jennifer Layer** is constantly chasing dreams and bringing everyone she can along for the ride to a more peaceful, graceful, and fulfilling life. When she's not working (or napping), the young author can be found climbing the sandstone cliffs in Utah, lost somewhere in the Appalachian Forest with her dog, enjoying a yoga class in the humid Houston summer with her friends, or training for her next ridiculous athletic race. She holds an undergraduate degree in Political Science and Communication Studies from Southwestern University and is currently getting her master's degree in Social Work from the University of Houston.

For updates on new, awesome stuff she's doing and creating:
Follow her on Instagram: **@jennyslayer**
Sign up for her email list by visiting
www.kindofcathartic.com